Clouds
of War

Clouds of War

PAST, PRESENT AND ON THE HORIZON

JERRY L. BURTON

Library of Congress Control Number:		2020914202
ISBN:	Hardcover	978-1-6641-2173-7
	Softcover	978-1-6641-2172-0
	eBook	978-1-6641-2171-3

Print information available on the last page.

Rev. date: 08/10/2020

To order additional copies of this book, contact:
Xlibris
844-714-8691
www.Xlibris.com
Orders@Xlibris.com
808970

Contents

Mary Lou (Maloney) Drumm

A wonderful wife, mother, and grandmother to her family, she was a gifted source to coworkers, a brilliant mathematician to her teachers, a cum laude graduate, and a delightful companion to her friends.

I miss you, Mary Lou.

August 16, 1925–February 13, 2014

FOREWORD

This book is more than just a biography. It is a history lesson through the eyes of a retired military combat veteran who served during World War II, the Berlin Crisis, the Korean War, the Cuban Missile Crisis (at the Pentagon), and in Vietnam.

> *Those who don't know history are destined to repeat it.*
> —Edmund Burke, 1729–1797

That's a nice saying and one that is probably near the top of the "has been quoted" list. At its core, it is true. However, when a person passes judgment on the events of history as good or bad, then cultural norms play a role in the way that history is interpreted and subsequently recorded.

There are many other factors as well, for example, the ability or inability of the observer of an event to have determined or influenced the historical outcome. Another element that may contribute to distortion of the documentation of a particular event, particularly if the outcome was not a desired one for the observer, is personal bias.

Even eyewitness accounts often vary considerably. With the passage of time, the accounts may conflict even more because of the personal differences of the witnesses. It's not that they lie. It's that the mind has a nasty habit of filling in the blanks. The data supplied by the mind can vary radically between individuals, even "identical" twins.

As an author, I have attempted to portray history in a scholarly way. I have performed extensive research and compared multiple sources. I have qualified the material used by citation. However, I cannot attest to the "truth" of the history I cite. Furthermore, I consider almost all historical accounts, particularly concerning human behavior and motive, to be skewed by human nature and cultural values.

Much of the history in this book was not personally witnessed by the lead character, William H. Drumm Jr. Yet that history, even before he was born, affected many events in his personal life. We are influenced by the history that preceded us, just as we will influence generations to come. I have attempted to blend into Bill's life story events that occurred a generation or more before he was born, events that have had a direct impact on who and what Bill would become. Bill's recounting of these events is heavily influenced by his father's generation and their interpretation of those events.

While accuracy and truth are major goals in this writing, I also try to explain the contrasts between views developed from different vantage points. Consider the contrast between the views of a conflict between the individual soldier, sailor, or airman who is involved in a small part of a much larger operation. The experiences of the individual under fire will vary greatly from that of the commanders who are observing the operations as a part of a greater plan and attempting to direct the overall operation.

Fog of war is another phenomenon that I try to address. Fog of war generally results from a lack of information pertaining to the importance of an operation. The goal may be clear, but the value of success may be clouded. When the battle begins and the bullets start flying, the fog of war increases. Bullets, bombs, rockets, and grenades can be very distracting. Under the stress of battle, the sense of situational awareness becomes clouded. Attention is drawn to the most immediate perceived threat. The most immediate perceived threat may not be the most immediate actual threat. The immediate goal becomes fight and survive regardless of what the higher goal might have been. Even after the battle has subsided, the warrior may not understand the importance of his or her actions. Limited information usually results from a need for secrecy or poor communications or high-threat conditions. Often things don't make sense based on the pieces you know. The point is made in Alfred Lord Tennyson's famous poem "The Charge of the Light Brigade,"

> Theirs not to reason why,
> Theirs but to do and die.[1]

Life for most people moves from generation to generation. Bill's life is defined by his dedication and service to his country. World history seems to move from war to war. So that is the course I have followed in recording the life of Ret. Lt. Col. (USAF) William H. Drumm Jr., MBA.

Ret. Lt. Col. (USAF) Jerry L. Burton, PhD

CHAPTER 1

World War I 1914–1918
(The Great War)

I, BILL DRUMM, was not born until after World War I. Yet that war, to a large degree, had already predetermined who and what I would become.

In the century before I was born, Empirical Europe was driving change in the world. Empires, by nature, are competitive. Competition creates tension. Tension can be resolved by war or compromise. Empires tend to choose war. So let's identify the key players on the stage and four factors that drove these great empires on a path toward war.

FACTOR 1: COMPETITION

At the turn of the century, the great empires were the Ottoman, British, German, Austro-Hungarian, French, and Russian empires. The Ottoman Empire had been at its height during the fifteenth and sixteenth centuries and was near the end of its long, slow decline. By 1922, it had disappeared altogether. Its remnants were the Turkish Republic and various Southeastern European and Middle Eastern states.[2]

The British Empire had become the largest empire to ever exist. But now, although still the major world power, its position was beginning to be threatened.[3]

The German Empire had been born on January 18, 1871. Before that, it was a loose confederation of German-speaking states. Germany as a nation-state grew very strong very quickly. By 1900, Germany had the best standing army in the world and one of the fastest-growing navies.[4]

The Austro-Hungarian Empire was formed in 1867 by the combining of the Austrian Empire and the Hungarian Empire. The Austrian Empire had exercised a great deal of cultural influence in European matters until its defeat by Napoleon's army in 1805. In an attempt to recover its influence, the Austrian Empire combined, in 1867, with its neighbor and strategic partner, Hungary. Thus, the Austro-Hungarian Empire was formed. In 1908, the empire annexed its neighbor, Bosnia-Herzegovina. This was a state of disparate nationalities. The Bosnian Serbs represented a majority and had hoped to become a part of Serbia, not Austria or Hungary.[5]

The French Empire consisted of colonies in North America, Africa, and Southeast Asia by the mid-1800s. Its territorial wealth was second only to Great Britain.[6]

The Russian Empire was a very diverse, multinational state founded by Peter the Great in 1721. In 1906, the "legislative" power was transferred to the State Duma.[7] The Duma was a significant step of transition from a monarchy toward a representative government, even though the Duma had no real legislative power. It was purely an advisory body.

One of the problems the Russian Empire had involved its military. Control of the seas was critical for military operations. Russia had no warm water ports. So during their cold winter months, their navy was either landlocked or dependent on foreign harbors.[8] Russia had to contract with Manchuria for a warm-water port.

In addition to the "great" empires, there were several countries that were striving to become great empires. Before 1840, China had been a closed society.[9] China's prominence as a nation, or empire, was based largely on trade with the United States. China began to lose its prominence after the United States opened trade with Japan in 1853.

Because of its wealth of natural resources in Manchuria, China had become the target of other empires, particularly the Japanese, Dutch, German, British, French, and Russian Empires. Because of trade with the United States, Japan quickly became industrialized. When China and Japan came into conflict in the Sino-Japanese War (1894–1895), Japan surprisingly emerged the victor.

Japan had hoped their victory over the Chinese would gain them "empire" status. It didn't happen.

Italy was another nation seeking "empire" status. The city-state of Rome was at one time a world empire, but it had become unrecognizable as an empire at least 400 years earlier. Some scholars believe it "disappeared" 1,400 years earlier.[10] Italy as a nation-state didn't even exist until 1861, when all the divisions of the area we now call Italy came together under one ruler. So by 1900, the nation of Italy was barely 30 years old! Italy was a new nation, weak and vulnerable, but with a rich empirical past.

The competition among the various empires was for, of course, power and prominence. Because the end justified the means, the competition took the form of an arms race among the empires.

FACTOR 2: METHOD OF GROWTH

The second factor leading toward war involved the "method of growth" of an empire. Growth in terms of territory involved invasion or colonization. Countries could be colonized by a conquering power or by a wealthy power contracting with the government of the weaker nation.

A major problem with colonization was that it generally resulted in the exploitation of the weaker partner. The stronger partner usually benefited far more than the weaker partner. The greater partner received the other country's natural resources, commerce, cheap labor, and sometimes food products, which are the things that strengthen and advance a country on the world stage. Meanwhile, the lesser country barely received subsistence. There's rarely anything in the deal for lesser country that would advance that country's standing in the world.

There might also be a protection clause for the weaker country. However, this was just another way to subordinate the weaker country to the stronger one.

Differences in race, language, and culture between an empire and its colony could potentially create animosity between the two. Animosity is often a trigger for rebellion.

FACTOR 3: INDUSTRIALIZATION

The third factor was industrialization. Empires enjoyed esteem and influence in the world community. But in the end, it was an empire's ability to force, if necessary, its influence on the world community that mattered. For example, the Austrian Empire had perhaps the highest level of cultural influence than any other country in Europe. Vienna alone influenced greatly the music, art, and cuisine of the rest of Europe. However, Austrian influence was of a gentile nature rather than of brute force power.

To receive greater esteem as a world power, the Austrian Empire combined with the Hungarian Empire to form the Austro-Hungarian Empire. Its quest for recognition as a military power later led to World War I.

The ability to pursue a strong military is dependent upon a strong economy. The industrial revolution brought about changes in manufacturing, transportation, weaponry, medicine/health, and futuristic vision. These are the reasons this period of advancement, "the Industrial Revolution," was referred to as a revolution! It literally changed most of the world—for better or for worse.

Certain critical elements are required to create industrialization. Having skilled and capable laborers, of course, is important. But in time, they can be developed. The most critical factor is natural resources. A country either has them or has to obtain them from an external source.

In the late 1800s, industrialization was occurring quickly, and a country without its own natural resources could not stay in the competition very long. This became a major source of friction among Russia, Japan, and China as we will see later.

Factor 4: Nationalization

The fourth factor leading to World War I was nationalism. This was often an offshoot of colonization or forced integration. In today's world, we tend to identify nations by their geographical boundaries. In Europe, it is apparent that the early idea of a "nation" of people was based on language and culture shared by the people of an area as much or more than the recognition of a natural or conceived geographical boundary. This concept played strongly in the events leading to World War I and to the attitude and actions of Hitler during the interwar period.

The forced integration of Bosnia-Herzegovina with the Austro-Hungarian Empire is an example of violating the language and cultural norms of a group of people. Austria-Hungary was "growing" its empire by appending other territory to their own. Serbia had been "courting" Bosnia, hoping that Bosnia-Herzegovina would join with Serbia to form a Slavic nation, much like Yugoslavia when it existed. That would have been a more natural merger because of their shared language and culture. The majority of the people in Bosnia-Herzegovina were Serbs.

The Young Turks movement in 1908 overthrew what was left of the Ottoman Empire in Bosnia. They were seeking independence, leading to a union with Serbia.[11]

However, the Serbs were a very strong nationalistic culture. To have an expanded Serbia would have been a major threat to Austria-Hungary. So Austria-Hungary preempted Serbia by annexing Bosnia-Herzegovina.

PRELUDE TO WAR AND THE FALL OF THE EMPIRES

On June 28, 1914, Archduke Ferdinand, the heir to the throne of Austria-Hungary, visited Sarajevo, Bosnia. He was trying to gain the approval of the Bosnian-Herzegovinian people. His pregnant wife, Sophie, rarely accompanied him on official visits. However, she was with him on this trip. A Serbian assassin shot and killed both the Archduke and his pregnant wife.

Austria-Hungary quickly checked with Germany to make sure their "mutual defense" pact would be honored by Germany if war broke out with Serbia. Germany assured Austria-Hungary it would.

After consulting closely with the Germans, the Austro-Hungarian Empire issued an ultimatum to Serbia. The ultimatum contained demands that clearly would be unacceptable to Serbia. The German-Austrian intent was that Serbia would reject the ultimatum. Austria-Hungary would then invade and quickly defeat the Serbs and append their territory to the Austro-Hungarian Empire.

What should have been a regional problem that was resolved between Austria-Hungary and Serbia became a European problem because of alliances.

JERRY L. BURTON

1. Austria–Hungary was allied with Germany.
2. Serbia was allied with Russia.
3. France and Britain were allied with Russia.
4. Britain was also an ally of Belgium.

You can see the chain reaction.

1. Austria–Hungary declared war on Serbia.
2. Russia was then obligated to declare war on Austria–Hungary.
3. Germany then was obligated to declare war on Serbia and Russia.
4. France then declared war on Germany.
5. When German troops took a "shortcut" through Belgium to attack France, Britain declared war on Germany.

Now you have every European Empire in the dog fight. Only one thing was missing. That was the Empire "Want a Be," Italy. Militarily, Italy was very weak. Italy could easily be swallowed up by either Germany or Austria–Hungary. So as a defensive move, they had joined the alliance between Germany and Austria–Hungary.

When the war broke out, Italy did not join the fight. She waited to see who looked like the winner and entered the war in 1915 on the side of Britain, France, and Russia.[13] Italy's contribution to the war was minimal, as you might expect. But it was a smart move on Italy's part because it placed them on the "winners'" side of the table at Versailles.

THE UNITED STATES AND NEUTRALITY[14]

The United States was providing funding and war supplies to both Great Britain and France as early as January 1, 1914.

The mood of the United States population was to remain neutral. One reason for this was that the immigration demographic in America at the time was divided between large segments of Anglos and Germans. Another reason was that the United States was heavily invested in the economies of Britain and France. If the Allies lost the war to Germany, the United States would not be able to collect the large sums of money that Britain and France owed them.

There were two major events that pushed America into the war. First, Germany refused to limit their submarine warfare to noncivilian targets. They agreed several times not to attack passenger vessels, but they failed to keep those agreements. Public opinion started to shift against Germany.

The other event was one that occurred in secret. The British intelligence had intercepted a telegram from the German government to their ambassador in Mexico. The contents of the telegram revealed

1. Germany's intent to renew unrestricted submarine warfare, and
2. Germany's intent to form an alliance with Mexico and Japan in the event that the United States declared war on Germany.

THE UNITED STATES ENTERS WWI

On April 2, 1917, President Wilson called on Congress to declare war on Germany.[15]

On April 6, 1917, the United States declared war on Germany.[16]

THE AMERICAN CONTRIBUTION[17]

The United States had hoped to stay out of the fighting part of the war. Not wanting to provoke Germany or give false hope to the British and French by building up the American military, they found themselves unprepared to engage in a war. The number of men in the U.S. Army and National Guard combined was about 370,000. A draft was instituted, and the military grew to 4.8 million men in all branches of the service by the end of the war. At war's end, the number of U.S. servicemen in Europe had grown from 300,000 to 1.4 million.

As early as January 8, 1918, President Wilson had drafted a proposal for peace—"The Fourteen Point Plan". It would allow for the secession of hostilities, withdrawal of troops, reasonable reparation penalties on Germany, and creation of a new mediation body to be known as the League of Nations.

On October 5, 1918, after the failure of Germany's Spring offensive, the Germans sent a telegram to President Wilson requesting that he intervene and take the necessary actions to restore peace according to his fourteen-point plan. President Wilson agreed, with the following conditions:

1. Germany had to retreat from all occupied territories.
2. Germany had to cease all submarine warfare.
3. The Kaiser had to abdicate his position.

On November 11, 1918, the armistice was signed. This marked the end of the war on the Western Front.

CASUALTIES OF WORLD WAR I[18]

German losses:	1.8 million	
Russian losses:	1.7 million	
French losses:	1.4 million	
Austria-Hungary:	1.2 million	
British losses:	950,000	
American losses:	48,000 killed in battle	56,000 lost to disease

WORLD WAR I WAS PERSONAL TO ME

I had three relatives in World War I: my father, William H. Drumm Sr.; my father-in-law, Luther G. Maloney; and my aunt Sadie A. Krause.

My father and father-in-law were drafted into the Rainbow Division. The Rainbow Division was the "brainchild" of Maj. Douglas MacArthur. The United States had not wanted to be involved in WWI if they could stay out of it. However, in April 1917, the United States declared war on Germany.

THE BIRTH OF THE RAINBOW DIVISION[19]

The United States needed to get 27,000 troops to France as quickly as possible. Pres. Woodrow Wilson mobilized approximately 122,000 National Guardsmen. However, they were not combat trained, and that would take time. The New York and Pennsylvania Guard Units were Division size. New York had just returned from active duty along the Mexican border, so they were combat ready and deployable immediately. However, the War Department did not want a state unit to be the first division sent to France. This is when they passed the problem down to Major MacArthur.

MacArthur suggested taking Guard Units from across the country and combining them into one division. He described it to his superiors and to the news media as being a division that would span the country like a "rainbow."

The vision caught on, and it became known as the Rainbow Division. It was made a part of the New York National Guard that, having been deployed recently, became the primary trainers for the new Division. The participating Guard Units were told to report to Camp Mills on Long Island on August 20. The Division was given the number 42.

COMPLETION OF TRAINING AND DEPLOYMENT[20]

The Rainbow Division was not the first but was one of the first American Divisions to reach the Western Front in November 1917. They first saw action fighting alongside the French in February 1918.

My father, William H. Drumm Sr. was drafted and sent to Long Island for training. Upon completion of his training, he was a private assigned to Company C, 106th Field Signal Battalion. He deployed to France from Brooklyn, New York, on October 7, 1918, on the Troop Transport vessel *Euripides*.[21] His commanding general was Maj. Gen. LeRoy S. Lyon. Once in France, the members of his unit were dispersed to fill vacancies in other units.[22] At the end of hostilities, he returned from Brest, France, on April 17, 1919, via the Troop Transport *Huntington* as a private first class in Headquarters Company 151st Field Artillery. He docked in Brooklyn, New York, on April 26, 1919.[23]

My father-in-law, Luther G. Maloney, was sent to Long Island for training. Upon completion of his training, he was a private assigned to Company A, 140th Regiment of Infantry. He deployed to France from New York, New York, on April 25, 1918, on the Troop Transport vessel *Adriatic*.[24] In France, his unit was trained by the British in June 1918. In July, they engaged in raids against the Germans in the Vosges Mountains. In September, they moved into the Saint Mihiel sector as a backup for the First Army. Next, they participated in the Meuse–Argonne offensive. This action was the largest battle the American Expeditionary Forces engaged in during the war. After five days, they were relieved and were placed in the Sommedieue Sector along the west face of the St. Mihiel salient, where they launched harassing attacks on the Germans until the armistice was signed on November 11, 1918.[25] He returned from Brest, France, on December 15, 1918, via the Troop Transport *George Washington* as a corporal in Headquarters Company 151st Field Artillery. He docked in Hoboken, New Jersey, on December 23, 1918.[26]

My aunt Sadie Anastasia Krause, my mother's sister, served in France during World War I as a nurse in the Army Nurse Corps. I don't know how she received her nurses training, whether it was in the Army Nurse Corps through the Red Cross or through another formal training program. In any case, she was one of the thousands of nurses who eventually went to Europe during World War I.

Planning Medical Support for AEF (American Expeditionary Forces)[27]

The War Department had acted early on getting hospitals and medical bases into France prior to the first U.S. combat troops. The effort actually began in 1916 when American civilian hospitals were "linked" with six military reserve hospitals for the purpose of building medical teams to go to Europe in the event that the United States entered the war. By the time the United States entered the war, the plan for constructing medical facilities in France was already developed. Logistics problems had been foreseen, and plans were in place to deal with these problems before they occurred.

In May 1917, the War Department asked the American Red Cross to mobilize these six military reserve hospitals for immediate shipment to France to work with the British Expeditionary Forces.

Deployment of the Medical Network[28]

The medical plan was to have major hospital centers strategically placed throughout France. There would be eleven of the hospital centers, known as territorial sections. Some of these sections would be placed near the ports. These would be called base sections. Other sections would be placed closer to the combat areas. These would be called interior sections. Each hospital center would have associated "hospitals" around them, perhaps five or six outer hospitals per center hospital.

After being operational for a short time, it was observed that soldiers at the front lines were dying before they could get to the base sections, where major surgery and other services could be offered. As a result, the "interior sections" became the "intermediate sections," and smaller facilities moved out away from the hospital center and closer to the battle line. These became known as an "advance sections." Some of them were as close as one and a half miles from the hostile action. The medical teams suddenly became as vulnerable as the soldiers. But the seriously wounded soldiers could be triaged more quickly and more lives saved.

BASE HOSPITAL #60[29]

30

My aunt Sadie was assigned to Base Hospital #60. This hospital had been organized in early April 1918 in Georgia. It was then moved on April 14 to the base hospital at Camp Jackson, South Carolina, for training. On August 11, the unit was moved to Newport News, Virginia. On August 22, the "hospital" departed for Europe on the *Dante Aleghiers*, arriving at Brest, France, on September 3. After eight days of rest, they departed for their permanent station in the hospital center at Bazoilles-sur-Meuse, Vosges. Hospital #60 was an advance section. They arrived on September 15, 1918.

Bazoilles-sur-Meuse, Hospital #60, was housed in Type A Units and tents. Type A Units were wooden barracks with two rows of beds with the head of the bed against the wall and the foot of the bed in the center of the building. There was an aisle about the width of a bed in between the beds extended from the walls.

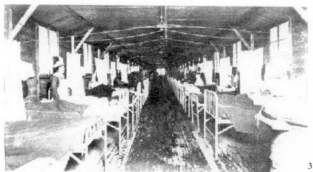

31

Type A Unit

Hospital #60 opened for patients on October 5. Sadie and her unit left for England on the *Lapland* on October 27, 1918. They arrived in Liverpool on November 8, 1918.[32] Apparently, they crossed England by rail and crossed the channel to France by ferry or by another national vessel. There is no record of a U.S. or U.S.-hire vessel transporting her to France.

There are records associating her with Hospital #60 even after the unit ceased operations. It is highly likely that she was moved to another operational unit and simply retained her original unit designation.

During its period of operation, Hospital #60 treated 3,684 medical and 2,304 surgical cases, with 334 operations. It ceased its operation on March 31, 1919. On June 15, the unit left from St. Nazaire on the *Texan*. They arrived back in the United States on June 29. The unit was demobilized at Camp Sherman, Ohio, on July 2, 1919.[33]

Aunt Sadie remained in France with other Army Nurse Corps nurses helping wherever they were assigned. On July 30, 1919, a group of them boarded a troop vessel, the *Leviathan*, and left Brest, France. They arrived in Hoboken, New Jersey, on August 6, 1919.

Aunt Sadie remained in the Army Nurse Corps for at least another eighteen months. There is a troop vessel record of her sailing from Antwerp, Belgium, on January 11, 1921, and arriving in Hoboken, New Jersey on January 23, 1921. She had told me some of her experiences in Europe. I remember her saying that she and some other nurses had seen Belgium and Italy. Undoubtedly, that was after the war had ended.

Sadie A. Krause
US Army Nurse Corps

JERRY L. BURTON

THE CONSEQUENCES OF WWI

The day after Britain had declared war on Germany, they asked Japan, an ally of Britain since 1902, to provide "limited naval assistance"[34] in locating armed German merchant ships. The benefit to the British was that this would allow the British fleet to remain in Atlantic waters near the fighting in Western Europe. This would be a benefit for the Russians because it would allow them to focus on the Western Front with Germany without worrying about an attack from the German installations in the Pacific. For Japan, it was an invitation to take control of East Asia and the Pacific.

The Japanese took the liberty of increasing their level of involvement to include seizing the German interests in the South Pacific and Indian Oceans as well as the German colonies in China, the Marianas, the Caroline, and the Marshall Islands.[35]

Furthermore, Japan issued "21 Demands" to China. Not all these were met, but the demands did result in Japanese control of the German holdings, Manchuria, and Inner Mongolia and various other mineral and mining complexes.[36]

China itself was neutral until August 14, 1917, when it declared war on Germany. The main objective of China was to regain some or all the territory it lost to Japan during the war. The land in question had been Chinese facilities leased to the Germans before the war.

In the end, Japan kept control over Germany's economic possessions in Shantung, including railways, mines, and the port at Tsingtao. Shantung was returned to China in February 1922.[37]

THE WINNERS AND THE LOSERS

At Versailles, the treaty declared Germany the loser. The allies—France, Great Britain, Italy, and the United States—were the "winners."

Punishment for Germany would occur in three areas: demilitarization, loss of territory, and economic constraints.

France wanted extreme penalties for Germany in every category.

Great Britain thought it critical that Germany be allowed to rebuild so that it would become a strong trading partner in the European community, particularly with Great Britain.

Italy just wanted to elevate themselves in the community of Big Powers and to rebuild the Roman Empire as it were. Italy made absurd territorial demands that were objected to by the United States.

The United States Congress viewed the Treaty of Versailles as a sham and refused to ratify it. So the United States was not a signatory.

In summary, the Versailles Treaty did the following to Germany:

1. Required Germany to sign a document stating that they were solely responsible for the war
2. Awarded 13 percent of its European territory and 10 percent of its people to other nations; much of the forfeited territory was inhabited by German-speaking people[38]
3. Demilitarization and occupation of the Rhineland
4. Forfeit all of its overseas possessions
5. Turn over the management of its industrial region to the League of Nations for fifteen years
6. Drastically reduced the size of the standing military
7. Denied the possession of an air force
8. Required reparations to be paid totaling more than thirty-three million in U.S. dollars, a sum that nobody expected Germany to pay in full[39]

So the big loser was Germany. The winning nations received reparations for their war efforts but not all that was promised.

So who was the BIG winner? JAPAN!

Japan got land and access rights to natural resources and industrial areas. Their empire expanded, and they were positioned to be the unchallenged top dog in the Far East.

AFTERMATH

Germany had been brought to its knees by the Treaty of Versailles. The stage was set for a former Bavarian lance corporal, Adolf Hitler, to become a Nationalist dictator and to start a real world war two decades later.

Russia, an ally of the French and Great Britain, had her hands full internally with a revolution, which began before WWI even ended.

Meanwhile, Japan, an ally of Great Britain, began seizing German colonies in China and the Pacific. A decade earlier, Japan secured a great deal of control over Manchuria and other parts of China. Japan needed natural resources to improve its military and general well-being. This need for natural resources drove Japan to enlarge its empire.

So at the end of WWI, there was a madman with a grudge in Germany and an emperor in Japan who was still seeking respect and was motivated by a shortage of natural resources to enlarge his empire.

I believe that the way WWI was settled by the "diplomats," particularly the French, made WWII inevitable.

CHAPTER 2

Between The World Wars
In The United States

T HE 1920S, OF course, was known as the Roaring '20s.
The war in Europe was over, the economy was booming,
and people in the cities had high hopes for a bright future. This
attitude was reflected in a popular song written by Irving Berlin
halfway through the '20s, "Blue Skies."

Blue skies smiling at me
Nothing but blue skies do I see[40]

THE ROARING '20S IN THE UNITED STATES[41]

The general population in the United States probably experienced
more change during the 1920s than any other decade before it.

During this decade, the economy roared. It grew a whopping
42 percent. The United States produced most of the world's goods.
That was made possible because much of the production capacity of
the rest of the world had been destroyed by the war.

Construction almost doubled; except for 1920–1921,
unemployment was at or below 4 percent. Average income rose from

$6,460 to $8,016 except for farmers. Every segment of the economy had expanded except farming.

Farming fell from 18 percent to 12.4 percent of the overall economy. Farmers suffered. Their taxes increased 40 percent per acre, while income fell 21 percent. By the end of the decade, the average annual income for farmers was $273!

GOVERNMENT, LAW, AND ORDER

The Eighteenth Amendment was passed on January 16, 1920. It was popularly known as prohibition. The legislation was well intended, but any good that had been anticipated was overshadowed by the crime wave that followed.

Organized crime flourished as bootlegging, and speakeasies became normal businesses. Notable criminals of the decade were Al Capone, "Bugs" Moran, Bonnie and Clyde, John Dillinger, George "Baby Face" Nelson, George "Lucky" Luciano, and George "Machine Gun Kelly" Barnes.[42] In 1929, members of Al Capone's gang executed seven members of Bugs Moran's gang in what became known as the St. Valentine's Massacre. My hometown of Chicago was the center of much of the nation's crime activity.

On August 18, 1920, the Nineteenth Amendment was ratified, giving women the right to vote. It seems that other "rights" quickly followed. Skirts got shorter, knee-high, and so did hair, introducing the "bob." It became fashionable for women to enter nightclubs without escorts and to indulge in smoking and drinking. The new word for these women, "flapper", entered the vocabulary. The *Charleston* was the rage of the dance scene.

Amid the roaring of the '20s, there were some "sober" moments. It was during this decade that the remains of an unidentified American soldier from World War I were laid to rest in the Tomb of the Unknown Soldier at Arlington National Cemetery. Then in late May 1922, the Lincoln Memorial was dedicated.

Legislation was also passed, granting citizenship to all Native Americans who had been born within the territory of the United States. The legislation was the Indian Citizenship Act.

By 1924, America was the place everyone wanted to go. Immigration had increased 15 percent since the last census, and the population of the United States topped 106 million people.

BILL DRUMM WAS BORN

I was born in Chicago on April 3, 1924. My parents, William Henry Drumm Sr. and Mary, had three children: me; my younger brother, Robert H.; and my younger sister, Marilyn Woolweaver. Both Bob and Marilyn are deceased.

My parents, William and Mary, were thirty-one and twenty-nine, respectively, when I was born. We lived about ten city blocks north of Soldier Field and about six blocks west of Lake Michigan at 1315 W 98th Street.

SCIENCE, TECHNOLOGY, AND INDUSTRY

Scientific and technological breakthroughs affected many, if not all, walks of life.

Communication, entertainment, marketing, and travel were all changed dramatically by the electrical grid, radio, "radio-vision," home appliances, airplanes, automobiles, and the creation of business machines.

To meet the increased demand for electricity on the West Coast and parts of the American Southwest, Congress approved the construction of Boulder Dam. The dam was later renamed Hoover Dam.[43]

My parents' generation was the first to benefit from all this new technology. It was life-changing.

The world "got smaller" during the '20s. Charles Lindbergh made the first solo, nonstop transatlantic flight from New York to Paris. The government approved "Air Mail" service, which boosted the use of airplanes in transporting people and goods.[44] Between 1926 and 1929, the number of air travelers increased from 6,000 to 173,000. "Barnstorming" and "wing walking" had also become popular!

An invention in 1926 that boosted the nation's power standing in the world was Robert Goddard's liquid fuel rocket. Of course, this raised tensions among the other military powers in the world.

By the end of the '20s, 60 percent of homes (ten million) had a radio. Radio stations became the source of news, music, and weather. With the advent of the radio, the advertising industry began to expand. By the middle of the decade, radio had become a source of entertainment as well. The Grand Ole Opry made its debut on November 28, 1925.[45]

NBC, CBS, and BBC established permanent radio networks.

Vaudeville, melodrama, and other stage shows had been popular for years. But radio opened another venue for those entertainers.

The movie industry flourished as well. Motion pictures moved from silent films to synchronized sound within the decade. Motion pictures became not only a mode of entertainment but also a mode of advertising and news reporting.

By 1924, the film industry had moved from New York City to California and had become the nation's seventh largest industry. And so Hollywood was born.[46]

Big name producers appeared like Samuel Goldwyn, Louis Mayer, Warner Brothers (there were four of them: Harry, Albert, Samuel, and Jack), and Cecil B. DeMille. The fast-growing movie industry in California even drew foreign producers like Alfred Hitchcock and Fritz Lang.

Actors and actresses, whose names everyone knew, included Rudolph Valentino, Marlene Dietrich, and Charles Boyer. There were other actors and actresses who had already made a name for themselves in the preceding decade: Douglas Fairbanks, John Barrymore, Gloria Swanson, Mary Pickford, Charlie Chaplin, Buster Keaton, Lon Chaney, Greta Garbo, Lionel Barrymore, and Joan Crawford, to name just a few.[47]

Top comedians included the Marx Brothers, Stan Laurel and Oliver Hardy, Ed Wynn (father of Keenan Wynn), Mae West, W. C. Fields, Bert Lahr, Will Rogers, Buster Keaton, and a very young Bob Hope. Another entertainer popular in vaudeville was Harry Houdini.

One of the quickest wits in live performance was Will Rogers. Here are two of my favorite quotes from him:

"Be thankful we're not getting all of the government we're paying for."[48]

"With Congress, every time they make a joke, it's a law. Every time they make a law, it's a joke."[49]

I think those two statements are as true today as they were one hundred years ago.

Henry Ford, through his assembly-line strategy, introduced an automobile that the average man could afford. He also introduced the forty-hour workweek. By the end of the decade, 25 percent of families owned a car. And the total number of cars registered would exceed twenty-six million by the end of the decade.

The automobile industry spawned many supporting industries. The government, by the end of the decade, had spent $1 billion on roads, bridges, and traffic lights. This, of course, created new sectors of commerce in the form of motels, gas stations, and restaurants. Naturally, the banks and insurance companies saw the opportunity for them to grow their services.

While the railroads were still the major means of transporting people and materials, the automobile was providing a means of individual movement over long distances not before available. On November 11, 1926, Route 66 was officially commissioned as the major road from Chicago to Los Angeles. It would eventually include 2,448 miles of road. By the end of the year, only 800 miles of Route 66 were actually paved. For the next fifty years, people would be "getting their kicks" on Route 66! That route, of course, became one of the nation's best-known east-west arteries.[50]

The 1920 census showed that almost 70 percent of the population lived east of the Mississippi River. But because of the increased mobility, more than two million people moved from the farm to the cities, but only one million people moved out of the cities to the farm. Thus, the nation became less rural.

In 1927, the world "shrunk" a little more when the first transatlantic telephone call was made. The call from New York City to London was made via radio waves.[51]

We take television for granted as if it has always been around. But it was on September 7, 1927, when the first real television was invented by American inventor Philo Taylor Farnsworth. The complete electronic television system wouldn't be patented for another three years, on August 26, 1930. No, it wasn't realistic color, surround sound, and wall mountable. It looked more like a large radio console with a window in the front, with a small black-and-white image, and it took up one-third of a wall in the living room. However, it did sound like a radio and required a receiving antenna almost as high as a radio antenna.

In the area of international politics, the United States recognized Chiang Kai-shek's Kuomintang government as the legitimate government of China.[52] The United States had sided with the "Nationalist" leader against the rival Communist leader, Mao Zedong. Mao was openly Communist, and Chiang was openly anti-Communist, and we were hoping to see a democracy established in China. I was only four years old when this occurred. But eighteen years later, it would determine the role I played in World War II.

My childhood was a very happy time.

Bill (two years old) and Bernice (Dolly, three years old)

I was about two in the picture above. Bernice, my aunt Sadie's adopted daughter, just thought I was irresistible, I guess. Aunt Sadie had no children of her own. We called Bernice Dolly because when Aunt Sadie first saw her, she declared, "What a little doll!"

Bernice was about five, and I was about four in this picture. I guess I was a fan of the navy at the time. We grew up almost like brother and sister.

Times were good for us. I had a two-year-old little brother, Bobby. Dad had a good job with the telegraph company, and we were "worry-free."

A sign of things to come in America was the participation in 1928 of both a Socialist Party presidential candidate, Norman Thomas, who won 0.7 percent of the popular vote, and a Communist Party presidential candidate who won 0.1 percent.[53] The "insignificance" of the vote totals of the two parties, even added together, is very misleading. What the numbers do not reflect is the determination of these two parties to change America and to do it within the democratic structure of our constitution. Within twenty-five years, the insurgency plan of the Communist Party, their plan for replacing our representative form of government, was actually read into the *Congressional Record*.

SPORTS

Sporting events had been big in the '20s. Baseball was the great American pastime, Babe Ruth hit sixty-six home runs in 1927, Jack

Dempsey was the hero in the boxing world, and Jim Thorpe was the track and football icon.

A PERSONAL ENCOUNTER WITH WALT DISNEY

On October 16, 1923, Disney Studios was created.[54] Walt Disney was born in my hometown of Chicago in 1901. He and his family moved to Kansas City when Walt was nine. He went to Benton Elementary School.

After completing elementary school, Walt went to McKinley High School in Kansas City. He also studied at the Kansas City Art Institute and School of Design and the Chicago Art Institute.

When Disney was about seventeen, he joined the Red Cross and was sent to France for a year to drive an ambulance to help with the war effort.[55]

There were many things to like about Walt Disney, but one thing he did that touched me personally involved my future wife, Mary Maloney. She was from Kansas City and attended the same elementary school as Walt Disney. Walt was about twenty-five years older than Mary, so they went at different times.

When Mary was in the sixth grade at Benton, the school held a special assembly for the students. When the kids were all gathered and quiet, thirty-six-year-old Walt Disney walked out into the center of the gymnasium. There was a tripod with a flip chart pad and some markers. He asked the kids who their favorite cartoon characters were. As they answered, he started drawing each character and talked about how they came to be "movie stars."

I loved hearing Mary tell that story.

THE GREAT DEPRESSION

It was probably the new inventions in the 1920s that caused the rapid rise in manufacturing numbers. Real gross domestic product rose from \$687.7 billion in 1920 to \$977 billion just before the stock market crash in 1929.

The newfound wealth in the upper class and the rise of the middle class led the stockbrokers and bankers to make some critically poor policies. One such innovative policy allowed customers to buy stocks on margin. That is, the broker would loan 80–90 percent of the value of the stock to the investor who would only put up 10–20 percent. If the stock prices went up, they became millionaires, but if stock prices fell, as they did in 1929, they went bankrupt.

All banks were supposed to hold reserves, but only one-third of the nation's banks did. The other two-thirds depended on the first third of the banks to hold reserve cash. Turned out, they didn't.

The United States had a vested interest in the economic recovery of France and Great Britain. France and Great Britain owed a very large lend-lease debt to the United States. At the same time, the United States wanted Germany to recover because the United States saw Germany as a strong future economic partner.

The problem was that neither France nor Great Britain had an economy that could produce anything because of the war damage. No products meant no sales. No sales meant no money with which to pay back the United States. France and Great Britain were relying on Germany to pay its war debt to them. Then they, in turn, would make payments to the United States. The reason this didn't work was that France and Great Britain, but mainly France, physically controlled most of Germany's economic capability, and they were removing raw materials needed by Germany to rebuild their economy.

So the United States and America's banks decided to loan Germany money so they could recover economically and repay France and Great Britain. France and Great Britain would then rebuild their economies and repay the United States for its loans or at least the interest on the loans.

France, however, didn't want Germany to recover. They preferred to "punish" Germany out of existence. And they almost did. France occupied the main industrial areas such as Rhineland, where Germany's natural resources were. Not only did Germany go through a famine, but also many people froze to death during the harsh winter because France was exporting all of Germany's coal needed for heating homes.

Unable to resurrect their economy, Germany had to pass the U.S. money directly on to France and Britain. The French and British, in turn, used the American money from Germany to rebuild their economies and to repay some of the lend-lease obligations.

The United States kept lending and losing money. The interest rates were raised by the banks to slow down borrowing by stock speculators and the U.S. government.

In August 1929, the Great Depression began, and the economy began shrinking. In September of the same year, the stock market reached its peak. By September 3, the Dow Jones Industrial average was pushed to a new high, 381.17. Then on October 24, the markets crashed.

There would be no quick recovery.

A few investors saw early on what was happening and began to withdraw from the market. Then others wanted to sell but could do so only at terribly reduced prices. The losses suffered between 1929 and 1931 of an estimated $50 billion started the worst American depression in the nation's history.

THE DUST BOWL

Severe drought hit the Midwest and Southern Great Plains in 1930. Massive dust storms began in 1931. A series of drought years followed, further exacerbating the environmental disaster.

By 1934, an estimated 35 million acres of formerly cultivated land had been rendered useless for farming, while another 125 million acres, an area roughly three-quarters the size of Texas, was rapidly losing its topsoil.

Regular rainfall returned to the region by the end of 1939, bringing the Dust Bowl years to a close. The economic effects, however, persisted. Population declined in the worst-hit counties where the agricultural value of the land failed to recover and continued well into the 1950s.[56]

BILL ENTERED GRAMMAR SCHOOL

Of course, I was just starting grammar school in September 1930, so I really didn't know what was going on out in the world. My parents enrolled me at St. Margaret's Grammar School in Chicago. It was, of course, a Catholic grammar school for boys. Girls had their own schools. School was all about the three "Rs"—"readin'," "'ritin'," and "'rithmetic." Because we were a Catholic school, we had a fourth "R"—religion.

My days were happy and filled with play. Going over to Aunt Sadie's was always fun. She lived within easy walking distance, and of course, "Doll" was always fun to play with.

The picture below is of me at age seven, Bernice at age eight, and my younger brother, Bob, at age six. The picture was taken just before church on the Sunday of Bernice's first communion.

Life was still good for us, and we were well-kept and happy kids.

JERRY L. BURTON

We, of course, had homework and tests to keep us busy during the school year. After school, there was always some time to run around with friends on the way home from school and on weekends. In my day, a group of friends was referred to as a gang. The word was different then. We didn't carry guns and knives and rob people or make trouble. We were just a bunch of kids burning energy.

Summers were good. There was the beach on the lakefront and movies with the folks and birthday parties and baseball games.

Life wasn't too different for us except that we didn't have fancy toys, electronic games, or television, cell phones, and the internet like today's kids. Chores, odd jobs, paperboy, telegram delivery boy, etc.?

Occasionally, I would overhear Mom and Dad talking about the world situation and the economy, but most of it was hard for me to relate to.

When I was about ten years old and Bob was about nine years old, we joined the Paulist Choir in Chicago. It was directed by Father O'Malley. Both my brother and I are in the picture below. When people come over and ask about the picture, I point to myself in the picture and tell my guests, "That's me. I was young and good-looking then. Now I'm just good-looking."

The first Paulist Choir was formed in Chicago by Fr. William Finn. Sometime later, Father Finn was moved to New York City, where he founded the Paulist Choristers at the Church of St. Paul the Apostle in Manhattan. Leroy Wetzel replaced Father Finn as director. Fr. Eugene O'Malley, a former member of Father Finn's Chicago Paulist Choir, later replaced Leroy Wetzel as director. Father O'Malley was considered the inspiration for the character of the same name portrayed by Bing Crosby in two popular movies, *Going My Way* and *The Bells of St. Mary's*.

Father O'Malley had a concert in Chicago once a year, and all the proceeds were used to rent the Black Oak Resort in Wisconsin to get the boys off the streets of Chicago. All the boys would go up there, and we'd play baseball. It was the quietest baseball game you'd ever heard because Father O'Malley would not tolerate any yelling or screaming for fear you would damage your vocal cords. My brother and I were in the choir for about five years before my parents moved to Indiana.

I wasn't really aware of the hard times that had come upon the nation. My parents did a good job of shielding us from the hardships that they as grown-ups had to face.

I hadn't developed much interest in the war talk at this time either. I was still at an age of self-development and self-discovery. Who was I and what was I going to be when I grew up? And who was I in my community of friends?

All that changed when I finished grammar school and entered high school in September 1938. I attended Saint Leo's High School on the south side of Chicago for one year before moving to Indiana in the summer of 1939. In that one year of high school, I received history classes that opened my eyes to current events. History became relevant, and I fell in love with the subject.

The Interwar Period in the Rest of the World

The decade of the '20 was great for the United States. The United States fully emerged as a world leader during that time. However, the rest of the world did not do so well.

The story of Germany, Great Britain, France, Russia, China, and Japan between the World Wars was more a story of the emergence of new leaders in those countries and their attempt to bring about change that would improve conditions for the people of their country. In some cases, it was more for the personal power gain of the new leader than it was for the relief of the burden on the common citizen.

Germany, France, and Britain entered the interwar period in bad economic shape. Their countries had suffered the ravages of war. What they lost in four years would require more than twice that long to rebuild. This is because, first, they had to rebuild production facilities that had been literally destroyed. Second, they had to replace a skilled workforce that had also suffered huge losses. Finally, they needed money to accomplish this. The United States tried to facilitate their recovery during the '20s, but in 1929, that bubble burst.

Germany, of course, suffered the most after the war. The start of reparation payments to the Allies led to two years of extreme inflation. Their ability to help themselves was virtually nonexistent. The German economy was largely controlled by France and Great Britain, who had occupied Germany's industrial areas.

By the end of 1922, the German government was unable to make "cash" reparation payments. So the French invaded the valley of the Ruhr on January 11, 1923. This area was an important industrial area of Germany because of its supply of coal. The French hoped to remove the coal for their own industrial use. The Germans had been trying to use it for domestic heating of homes during the winter. It was August 25, 1925, before the French withdrew from the region.[57]

During this time, Adolf Hitler became politically active. Most people think that Hitler formed the Nazi Party. He didn't. The Nazi Party had been formed by a worker's group that was opposed to the Communist movement in Germany. I think that was around 1920.

Hitler joined it in 1921 and soon became its leader.[58] Between that time and 1925, Hitler was imprisoned twice for violent activities and treason. He used his time during his second prison term to dictate the first volume of *Mein Kampf*.[59]

In April 1924, the United States presented the Dawes Plan that would require France to withdraw from the Ruhr valley. It also restructured the reparation payment schedule for Germany.[60]

Hitler quickly rose to prominence and, by 1934, when President Hindenburg died, had achieved dictatorial power. With his new power, he eliminated his enemies, political and ethnic.

Hitler's army and air force rushed to test their new legs and wings and weaponry in the Spanish Civil War, which began on July 17, 1936. Germany's involvement was veiled in the idea of helping Franco, a nationalist, stop the spread of Communism in Europe. By April 1939, when the Spanish Civil War had been decided in favor of Franco, Germany had supplied Franco with around sixteen thousand men and almost one hundred airplanes.[61]

The British and the French exercised restraint concerning involvement by the Germans in the Spanish Civil War because they too opposed Communism.

The Italians, during this interwar period, had tried to look like an emerging "empire" under Benito Mussolini. However, Mussolini failed to impress Germany or anyone else with his invasions of third-world countries.[62]

The Stalin Reign of the 1930s[63]

In 1922, Russia had become the Soviet Union. Lenin was a minority dictator and failed to accomplish much for the people of Russia. On his first day in power, he banned private ownership of land and nationalized industry. He made one attempt at introducing democracy, but when his party only received one-fourth of the assembly, he dissolved the assembly, banned all parties but his own, imposed strict censorship of the press, and declared that he would rule by force with no guidance from the people or from law. Subsequently, Lenin had thousands of his political opponents murdered. A failed assassination attempt in which Lenin was shot in the neck and shoulder contributed to his death several years late. Lenin had several strokes and finally died of a brain hemorrhage. Two years before his death, Lenin had appointed Stalin to the position of General Secretary of the Communist Party.[64]

Stalin was not fully accepted as Lenin's replacement until about five years after Lenin's death.[65] During this battle for acceptance, it became clear to him that he had to purge everyone who might be his enemy.

There were basically three things accomplished by Stalin:

1. Instituted the five-year plans
2. Instituted collectivism
3. Carried out the Great Purge

The "five-year plans" were hopes with no substance. Eventually, Stalin had to allow the collectivist farmers to produce enough food for themselves and their families and the ruling class, and then they could sell to other people for profit. Stalin claims there was no famine in 1932–1933, but there were reportedly at least 7.5 million Ukrainians who perished and at least 2 million Kazahks.[66]

The political goals were more "successful." The "Terror," as it was often called, began in 1934 and lasted until 1938. The process of purging enemies took the form of staged trials, outright murder, and execution. The secret police carried out much of this activity using torture of the accused and their relatives to force "confessions."[67]

Stalin even had three thousand of his Red Army executed. Stalin signed a decree that allowed children as young as twelve to be executed if their parents were thought to be disloyal to Stalin.[68]

Roughly one-third of the entire Communist Party's three million people were purged.[69] Gulag Labor Camps sprung up across the Soviet Union. Many who were sent to these camps were eventually executed.[70] An accurate count of the deaths is impossible to determine. But experts agree it was easily in the millions.[71]

Japan–China in 1920–1938[72]

During the 1920s, Japan suffered significant economic and political conflict. The two party system was being tried, and the Communist Party was trying to gain enough power to overthrow it.

Economically, Japan had suffered through the 1920s because of the amount they spent on their military during World War I. However, they made some economic gains through increased exports and did not suffer as deep a recession in the 1930s as the rest of the world.

Japan was less aggressive toward China during the 1920s despite the Communists in Japan who wanted to support the Communist revolution in China.

The United States and Britain were seeking a "status quo" in the Pacific and agreed not to build any new military bases between Singapore and Hawaii. The United States, Britain, Japan, France, Italy, Belgium, China, the Netherlands, and Portugal signed an agreement they hoped would prevent future war in the Pacific. The signatories agreed to respect China's independence and integrity and not to interfere in Chinese attempts to establish a stable government.[73]

Japan under Hirohito[74]

In the late 1920s, Emperor Hirohito was enthroned, and Japan began to move back toward a traditional Japanese society. The nation was still politically divided, and there was an unsuccessful assassination attempt on Hirohito. The nationalists began to consolidate power behind the emperor. Eventually, the internal conflict led to militarism.

A shortage of natural resources was still a limiting factor for Japan as it struggled to become a world power. So in 1931, Japan again invaded Manchuria. The sporadic fighting continued until it became an all-out war with China in 1937.

Little was done by the major world powers because they were trying to recover from WWI. The United States, Britain, France, and Russia were strong isolationists. Germany was just beginning to recover as a nation.

The United States cut back on its supply of oil to Japan in an attempt to back them away from their militarism. Instead, it turned Japan from an ally to an enemy.

Japan had been taking note of Germany's success with "blitzkrieg" attacks. Using that model, they began to plan an attack on the United States. The German model of "blitzkrieg" also inspired their future attacks on China.

By mid-December 1937, Japan was able to take Nanking, the Nationalist capital of China, in a brutal massacre referred to as the Rape of Nanking. Over three hundred thousand citizens of Nanking were raped, murdered, and some even buried alive.

In China, the Nationalists were led by Chiang-Kai-shek. Chiang leaned toward a free-enterprise system of society and was opposed by Mao Zedong, the leader of the Communist Revolution. However, by late 1936, Chiang and Mao called a truce between them. They recognized that the invasion of China by Japan was a greater threat than they were to each other, at least for the moment.

In the period following, the Japanese took control of virtually all the Chinese ports. However, outside the cities and the ports, the Japanese faced strong opposition from guerilla forces of both the Nationalists and the Communists.

The Japanese took control of French Indochina when France fell to Germany in 1940. Later, in 1942, when Germany was engaging Great Britain in the Europe theater, Japan was able to take control of Burma and shut down the Burma Road and all traffic from India to China. In effect, Japan had isolated China from the outside world.

As a result, Nationalist China fell into economic and social problems. Also, by this time, Japan was bombing many Chinese cities. China was on the verge of defeat, but Chiang refused to surrender or even negotiate with the Japanese. Meanwhile, the scattered areas controlled by Mao's Communist followers grew as a result of Chiang's weakened army and the lack of Japanese aggression against the Communist areas. The Japanese considered the Communists as insignificant since they were not consolidated geographically nor were they the official government of China.[75]

GERMAN AGGRESSION

During my last semester at Saint Leo's High School, on March 12, 1938, German troops entered German-speaking Austria and annexed it as part of the Third Reich.[76] That was a bit of bad news, but I also received a bit of bad news on a personal level. Because of the depression, we were losing our home, like so many people during that hard time.

My father was going to lose his position with the Western Union Telegraph Company, but they offered him a lower position as a lineman at $75 a month, and he would have to leave Chicago and work in Indiana. He accepted the position.

He and Mom acquired a piece of land at Fish Lake, about eleven miles southeast of La Porte. They also acquired a large number of cedar logs (telephone poles) and built a log cabin there at the lake. We had running water in the kitchen for as long as you could work the hand pump. We used kerosene for lighting, heating, and cooking. The "privy" was out back.

The Log Cabin My Father Built

I attended my sophomore, junior, and senior years of high school in the small town of Mill Creek (Lincoln Township), Indiana. I played center on the high school basketball team. My brother was the manager. He's in the back row, sweater and tie.

During my senior year, I worked as a hired hand on a farm. Our graduating class at Mill Creek totaled thirteen students. The high school population, grades 8 through 12, totaled only about two hundred. As a small school, it was hard for Mill Creek to compete for good math and science teachers. As a consequence, I would later find myself at a disadvantage when competing for a pilot position.

Life was different in the farmland. The school was "coed," boys and girls attending school together. I thought that was a great idea.

My daily routine was really different. The days began the same at home, but it was a five-mile walk to school, only two miles if I took the railroad tracks. Coming back each day, I stopped at the farm where I worked as a farmhand.

After work, I walked the rest of the way home and ate supper and did my homework.

On weekends, I worked at the farm. On Saturday nights, the famer, Charlie Wolf, would open his barn for square dancing. The music was provided by locals—we always had at least a violin and piano. Charlie did the "calling." We usually had three to four squares. When we all got going, it was "Katie bar the door"! I really loved to square dance.

During the summer, I worked on the farm. The farm grew peppermint. More than 10 percent of U.S.-grown peppermint is produced in Indiana.

A peppermint is roughly the size of a large head of cabbage or lettuce. It has to be weeded on your hands and knees. After cutting the peppermint, the leaves are washed, dried, and then distilled.

School was a bit more challenging. There were a lot of distractions. Travel time to and from school took a chunk out of my time.

During basketball season, I would do chores at the farm after practice. Then I would go home, eat, study, and do homework. I was one tired boy at the end of a day!

My senior year was easier because I lived on the farm.

Social life was very different. Interacting in a coed environment is more fun than in a single-gendered environment. For a teenage boy, it's far more distracting too.

One of my friends owned a Hudson Terraplane. He would take me and two other guys for joy rides on the country roads—at eighty miles an hour. You couldn't do that in Chicago!

Academically, it was much more challenging and interesting than grammar school. I really enjoyed the history. Because of my high level of interest in history, I became deeply interested in current events.

To me, as a high school student in 1939 entering my sophomore year, I began to see how the past and the present was shaping my future.

I began to understand and appreciate the involvement of my father and aunt in World War I. I also was able to see a trend toward another great power struggle in Europe and the Pacific.

JERRY L. BURTON

CHAPTER 3

Transition from Peace to War

THE MOOD OF American was that of isolationism. As I became aware of the actions of Germany, Italy, and Japan, I became disappointed with nations like Great Britain and France and even my own country for not breaking this chain of events before it led to another great war.

Then on September 3, 1938, it happened. Adolf Hitler, Benito Mussolini, French Premier Edouard Daladier, and British Prime Minister Neville Chamberlain signed the Munich Pact. It was obvious to me that Hitler signed it to keep the French and the British from interfering with his plans for further aggression. Mussolini signed it as a "want to be" riding on the coattails of a bully. France and Britain signed it believing that they could achieve "peace through appeasement." The deal sealed the fate of Czechoslovakia, virtually handing it over to Germany in the name of peace. Chamberlain returned to Britain and proudly declared that he had achieved "peace in our time."[77]

On August 23, 1939, the Nazi-Soviet Non-Aggression Pact was signed between Germany and the Soviet Union. This pact was a mutual promise between the two leaders that neither would attack the other. This pact was again instrumental in keeping the Soviet

Union, to the east of Germany, from being a threat to Hitler as he overran Western Germany. For this, Germany had promised the Soviet Union Latvia, Estonia and Lithuania, and half of Poland. However, on June 22, 1941, less than two years later, Hitler broke the pact by attacking the Soviet Union.[78]

On September 1, 1939, Germany invaded Poland. Adolf Hitler claimed it was a defensive action. The Germans executed a coordinated attack using aircraft, panzer tanks, infantry, machine gunners, heavy artillery, and German ships and submarines. On September 2, the British and French demanded that Hitler withdraw from Poland by the next day or face war. Hitler refused. The Second World War had begun![79]

WORLD WAR II[80]

The first full year of the war saw Germany invading its European neighbors: Belgium, the Netherlands, France, Denmark, Norway, Luxembourg, and Romania. The Germans bombed Britain for months. However, their hope of invade Britain failed because of their inability to gain air superiority.

The Royal Air Force undertook nighttime raids over Germany in response.

The news was everywhere. We heard it on the radio, read it in the newspapers, and saw it on the news reels at the movie theaters. Hitler was devastating Europe!

Meanwhile, Germany, Italy, and Japan signed a joint military and economic agreement on September 27, 1940,[81] thus forming the Axis powers. Then Italy invaded Egypt, which was controlled by the British. The invasion was only partially successful. Italy followed that invasion with invasions of Albania and Greece.

The United States shifted to a stance of "nonbelligerency" rather than neutrality so it could find ways to help the Allies. The Lend-Lease Act allowed the transfer of materiel aid to Great Britain in exchange for ninety-nine-year leases on property to be used by the

United States for foreign military bases. Popular opinion still didn't want Americans in another war "over there."

The Soviet Union meanwhile took part of Romania and installed Communists in the Baltic states, later annexing them.

As early as May 1940, the Germans established Auschwitz. It was several years before the Allies knew what was happening there.

On May 10, Germany invaded France, Belgium, and the Netherlands. Hitler didn't invite Mussolini to assist in the invasion because Italy was so ill-prepared for war they would have been a liability. The French and British armies thought a stalemate had been reached, but the Germans surprisingly broke through the Ardennes with tanks, flanked the French and British troops, and trapped four hundred thousand Allied troops against the sea at Dunkirk.

The German tank troops delayed their advance on the trapped Allies and held their positions to allow the German foot soldiers to catch up and join the attack. Hitler agreed to a two-day wait, hoping to maintain a net around the Allies and not allow them to escape.

On May 26, the evacuation of Allied troops from Dunkirk, France, began.

When Hermann Göring asked permission to use the Luftwaffe to destroy the trapped Allies, Hitler approved it.

The two-day delay turned into three days because of the bad weather delaying the progress of the foot soldiers. The weather also reduced the effectiveness of the air strikes.

British fighter aircraft attempted to stop the German bombers from reaching the beach. The Royal Air Force lost many fighters in the process.

Around 338,000 men were evacuated in four days. About 90,000 troops were left on the beach with tons of military equipment.[82]

On June 5, 1940, the German Luftwaffe began air strikes on channel ports and convoys. On June 10, Germany intensified the air strikes. Italy thought that Britain would certainly fall to the Germans soon. So hoping to be included in the "winners' circle," Italy hastily declared war on France and Great Britain.

Twelve days later, France surrendered to Germany. France was divided into a German-occupied zone, an area around Vichy that was allowed to represent the seat of the "free" French government and a small area just to appease the Italians. The area given to Italy became a haven for French Jews because Italian officers refused to arrest them and hand them over to the Germans.[83]

After Hitler had reduced France to a status of "irrelevant," the battle for Britain began. Hitler wanted to completely destroy the Royal Air Force. As long as the Royal Air Force existed, attempting an invasion had to be ruled out as impractical. The German army would have to load men and equipment aboard ships and cross the English Channel. The exposure of men and materials on a beach waiting to be loaded onto ships in docks would be like committing suicide in the face of enemy air power.

So elimination of the RAAF was a priority, and the task was given to Hermann Göring. He had hoped for this opportunity.

Between May 26 and June 4, 1940, the British Expeditionary Forces escaped from the European continent via Dunkirk. The British were unable to extract about ninety thousand fighting men and untold tons of tanks, artillery, and other military equipment. As a result, the German land and air forces significantly exceeded those of the British. So on June 5, the Germans began their air attacks on the English Channel ports and convoys.

On July 10, 1940, the British sent up RAAF airplanes to intercept the Luftwaffe, and the air battles known as the Battle of Britain began.

On July 16, 1940, Hitler instructed his army and navy to prepare for Operation Sea Lion, the invasion of Great Britain. Three days later, on July 19, Hitler, in a public speech, offered peace to Britain if they would allow him to dominate the European continent. The offer was rejected—Britain would continue to fight and "never surrender."

When the Germans intensified the bombing of the British ports and started including Britain's radar net and airfields, Great Britain bombed Berlin. This infuriated Hitler. The raids continued back and forth for approximately fourteen months.

Then on September 15, 1940, the back of the German Luftwaffe was broken. On that day alone, the Luftwaffe lost fifty-six aircraft in two dogfights in less than an hour. Four days later, Hitler discontinued "Operation Sea Lion."

However, in October, Hitler ordered massive bombing of British cities. He had hoped to discourage the people of Britain and force an early armistice. This plan did not succeed either. Hitler finally gave up the idea of conquering Britain in May 1941 and turned his attention to the USSR.[84]

On September 13, 1940, Italian forces invaded Egypt from Libya. Their goal was to gain control of the Suez Canal and secure the eastern end of the Mediterranean as well as gain access to the oil beyond. They had two hundred thousand troops compared with the British and Commonwealth army of only thirty-six thousand men. But General Graziani, leading the Italian forces, was not up to the task. The British stopped him.[85]

Unlike WWI, the United States anticipated having to go to war in Europe. So on September 16, the United States began its first peacetime draft.[86]

Still looking for a clear victory in battle, on October 28, 1940, Italy invaded Greece. They wanted to capture it before Hitler did. The Greeks, far more experienced in mountainous terrain warfare than the Italians, drove the Italians back to Albania.[87]

★ ★ ★ ★ ★

On November 5, 1940, Franklin Roosevelt had won an unprecedented third term as president. He had run on an isolationist platform, promising American families, "We will not send our Armed Forces to fight in lands across the sea except in case of attack."

Roosevelt had promised maximum aid to Great Britain while maintaining his promise not to send any American boys into the war in Europe. So when the British prime minister Winston Churchill asked Roosevelt for fifty mothballed WWI destroyers, Roosevelt sent them. In return, the United States received five bases in the Western hemisphere.[88]

I kept asking myself, "What are we waiting for? Innocent people are being killed, and the Nazi war machine keeps taking over country after country while giving only the weakest of excuses for doing so."

In December 1940, Australian, British, and Indian troops swept around the Italian Tenth Army in Operation Compass. The Tenth Army was cut off, and 130,000 Italians surrendered. The arrival of the German Afrika Korps under Rommel gave the Axis the edge again, and Italian troops participated in a second invasion of Egypt. But they, along with the Germans, were driven out once more in an operation named Operation Crusader.[89]

The year 1941 was one of escalation around the world. Greece was defeated by Germany, who then launched invasions of Yugoslavia and Russia. Germany broke its pact with the Soviet Union and invaded there, but the harsh winter and Soviet counterattack killed many German troops. The Soviets then joined the Allies.

Pearl Harbor, on December 7, 1941, the United States declared war on Japan. The next day, December 8, 1941, the United States declared the event an open act of war. So the war with Japan was on.

Hours later, the United States also declared war on Germany and the Axis powers. My thoughts were "It's about time!"

My father and aunt both served in World War I, my father in France with the Rainbow Division and my aunt, also in France, as a nurse.

On December 11, 1941, Germany and Italy declared war on the United States, and then the United States declared war on Germany and Italy.

IT WAS TIME FOR MY GENERATION TO STEP UP!

Between Pearl Harbor, on December 7, 1941, and December 27, 1941, less than three weeks, the Japanese were able to invade and capture almost every Pacific Island between Japan and Pearl Harbor. These islands included the Philippines, Wake Island, Guam, Malaya, and British Borneo.

In addition to the Pacific Islands, Japan was invading and occupying parts of Southeast Asia, including Thailand, Shanghai, Singapore, Burma, and Hong Kong.

They also bombed Manila and forced General MacArthur to begin withdrawal from Manila to Bataan.[90]

In Burma, Japan wanted to cut China off from the Allied Armies in India and Burma by capturing the Burma Road. The Burma Road was the only ground route between India and China, suitable for transporting supplies. The Japanese felt this isolation strategy would enable Japan to defeat China more easily.[91] China already controlled all of China's southern and eastern ports, including Hong Kong.[92]

Japan was dominating the Western Pacific islands.

CLOUDS OF THE PAST

As I looked back on the past decade, I saw a pattern that concerned me, my family, and most of my friends. In September 1931, Japan, seeking land acquisition and natural resources, invaded Manchuria. Their ultimate goal was the domination of China and the Far East. In short, it appeared they were seeking empire status.

In 1935, Italy invaded Ethiopia. Ethiopia was one of only two African countries that had not been colonized by a European power. The other African country was Liberia. By invading Ethiopia, Benito Mussolini sought to elevate his prestige and move closer to reestablishing the Roman Empire. His advantage in modern war machines, including the use of poisonous gas, allowed his invasion to succeed. I was only in the sixth grade in grammar school, but the horror of this event stuck with me and stirred my interest in history.

Germany had been rearming, and it looked like there could be war in Europe again. In response, Britain's Prime Minister Neville Chamberlin traveled to Munich, where he signed the

Munch Agreement on September 30, 1938. The agreement allowed Germany to annex the Sudetenland portion of Czechoslovakia on the basis that most of the inhabitants there were German-speaking. Hitler promised that this would be his last territorial claim.

Many, including myself, considered the Munich Agreement to be a sham. Eleven months later, on September 1, 1939, Germany invaded Poland to regain land they had lost during World War I.

CHAPTER 4

Growing Up

SIX MONTHS AFTER the Japanese attack on Pearl Harbor, I graduated high school and, from high school, entered St. Benedict's College in Atchison, Kansas, on a partial basketball scholarship. I was going to major in history. It was at St. Benedict's that I met my future wife, Mary Lou Maloney, at a freshman "mixer" dance. She was a student at another college across town, Mount St. Scholastica College for Women.

One of our favorite persons at St. Benedict's was Father Gilbert. He worked at both schools.

I was born and raised in Chicago as a kid. Racism against the blacks was horrible on the south side. My whole family was prejudiced against blacks. That, of course, influenced me when I was a kid. Mary Lou, on the other hand, didn't have any prejudice even in her little fingernail. When she heard me talking about the blacks, she just about went through the ceiling. So when we got back to school again, she got to Father Gilbert before I did, and she told him about my prejudice.

When I went in to get my course schedule, I was sitting there looking through my courses, and he came in and said sociology so and so. I responded, "I don't want that one." He said, "What?" I repeated, "I'd just as soon not take that sociology course." He said, "Bill, do you want to graduate from St. Benedict's?" I answered, "Yes, Father. Okay, sociology."

I was a changed person after that sociology course. I had not realized just how racist I was. I would like to see a sociology class, or some other class that covers race sensitivity, required in all high schools. Hopefully, schools have already made that step. When I returned to duty, I told my commander that I thought the military needed to require training in this area.

In November, recruiters from the army, navy, Army Air Corps, and marines came onto campus. They were interviewing all the freshmen, hoping to get enlistees. The army, navy, and marines were up front with us and told us that if we signed up with them, we could go at any time. They warned, "We might send you a letter next week."

Then there were the Army Air Corps guys. They were real sweet talkers! "We'll let you stay in school until you finish your second semester, and we won't call you until after that." They showed me where to sign, and I did. So on December 1, 1942, I was sworn into the Army Reserve Corps as part of the U.S. Army Air Forces Aviation Cadet Program.

Christmas came, and home I went to spend my vacation with my family. In January, after the break, I returned to school. Waiting there for me was a letter:

Dear Bill,

We'd like to have your presence at Jefferson Barracks, Missouri, to join the Army Air Corps as an Aviation Student.

So with only one semester of college, off I went to the Army Air Corps.

★ ★ ★ ★ ★

THE WAR IN EUROPE IN 1942

This time the United States was prepared for war. The first U.S. troops arrived in Britain in January 1942.

Although Germany had captured Libya, the Allies started making gains in Africa.

In Russia, Soviet counterattacks were making progress in Stalingrad. Back in Europe, the Battle of Stalingrad began on August 21, 1942.

THE WAR IN THE PACIFIC IN 1942

During the three months of 1942, the Japanese invaded Java in the Dutch East Indies, Sumatra in the Dutch East Indies, Bali, Java in the Dutch East Indies, Singapore, Sumatra in the Dutch East Indies, Salamaua and Lae on New Guinea, and the Andaman Islands in the Bay of Bengal.

The United States launched its first U.S. aircraft carrier offensive of the war on February 19 as the *Yorktown* and the *Enterprise* conducted air raids on Japanese bases in the Gilbert and Marshall Islands.

On February 23, 1942, the Japanese attacked the U.S. mainland. A submarine off the coast of California shelled an oil refinery near Santa Barbara.

On February 26, the United States lost its first carrier, the *Langley*. It was sunk by Japanese bombers. The next day, the Japanese engaged the United States in the Battle of the Java Sea. The Japanese prevailed and were successful in sinking the largest U.S. warship in the Far East, the *Houston*.

The Japanese, on March 4, 1942, bombed Pearl Harbor again, this time using two Japanese flying boats. At the same time, the aircraft carrier *Enterprise* attacked Marcus Island, just one thousand miles from Japan.

On March 7, 1942, the Japanese forced the British evacuation of Rangoon in Burma.

April began badly for the United States, when on April 9, 1942, Gen. Jonathan Wainwright was forced to surrender unconditionally the U.S. forces on Bataan to the Japanese. The next day, seventy-six thousand Allied POWs, including twelve thousand Americans, were forced to begin a sixty-mile walk under a blazing sun without food or water toward a new POW camp. Over five thousand American soldiers died in what became known as the Bataan Death March.

On April 18, 1942, the United States struck back as a flight sixteen B-25s launched from the deck of the aircraft carrier the *Hornet* bombed Tokyo. It was a one-way flight because of the limited range of the bombers. Little damage was done to ground targets, but the civilians in Japan realized that they were not untouchable. No aircraft were lost to enemy fire. The Japanese, on the other hand, lost five fighters.

Eleven days later, on April 29, the Japanese took Central Burma. Two days later, they occupied Mandalay in Burma.

May opened badly for the United States as the focus remained on the war in Europe. On May 6, 1942, the Japanese take Corregidor as General Wainwright was forced to unconditionally surrender all United States and Filipino forces in the Philippines.

However, as Japanese admiral Isoroku Yamamoto had suggested, six months to the day from Pearl Harbor, the United States prevailed. May 7–8 saw Japan suffer its first defeat of the war during the Battle of the Coral Sea off New Guinea. This was the first time in history that two opposing carrier forces fought only using aircraft without the opposing ships ever sighting each other.

On May 20, in the China Burma India Theater of operation, the Japanese completed the capture of Burma and reached India.

At the end of May, the Japanese attacked the U.S. carriers that had been "lured" to Midway. Their hope was that by capturing Midway, they could extend their defensive barrier and protect Japan against further air attacks like the Doolittle raid. U.S. cryptographers had broken Japanese communication codes and were able to make their own plans of attack. What resulted was the Battle of Midway, which lasted from June 3 to June 6.

As a diversion for the United States, on June 2, the Japanese launched a raid on Dutch Harbor, in the Aleutians. There was very little damage. On June 3, they again attacked Dutch Harbor, this time killing forty-three U.S. personnel. The Japanese destroyed eleven U.S. planes while losing ten of their own.

On June 6, the Japanese occupied Kiska, also in the Aleutians. The following day, they took Attu. There was no resistance to the Japanese on either island. The Japanese took forty of the citizens of Attu back to Japan, where they were interred. Twelve of the forty died of disease or starvation.[93]

Also on June 6, the Battle of Midway drew to a close. The defeat for Japan was catastrophic—4 carriers, a heavy cruiser, 320 planes, and approximately 3,000 Japanese sailors and airmen. Many of the airmen were Japan's top fliers. The United States lost 1 carrier, 1 destroyer, and nearly 150 planes, almost two-thirds of which were carrier-based. Only 317 sailors, airmen, and marines from the Midway garrison were lost.[94]

In August, the marines began a series of invasions to retake islands from the Japanese. It was important that the islands be recovered from east to west approaching Japan. That way, you're fighting in one direction with no enemy behind you. The priority was islands with existing or reparable airfields.

On August 7–8, the U.S. Marines began counterinvasion operations to recover the islands taken earlier by Japan. One of the first major battles was the first U.S. amphibious landing of the Pacific War. It occurred at Tulagi and Guadalcanal. The unfinished airfield on Guadalcanal was taken back and renamed Henderson Field. The Battle of Guadalcanal was not a short one. It was February 1943 before the Japanese evacuated the island.[95]

On September 9–10, 1942, a Japanese floatplane flew two missions, dropping incendiary bombs on U.S. forests in the state of Oregon. This was the only bombing of the continental United States during the war. Newspapers in the United States voluntarily withheld this information to avoid creating panic in America.

September was not looking good for the United States. On September 15, a Japanese submarine operating near the Solomon Islands sank the carrier *Wasp* and the destroyer *O'Brien* and damaged the battleship *North Carolina*.

October was looking better. On October 11–12, U.S. cruisers and destroyers defeated a Japanese task force in the Battle of Cape Esperance off Guadalcanal. The next day, the thirteenth, the first U.S. Army troops, the 164th Infantry Regiment, landed on Guadalcanal.

However, on October 14, the Japanese attacked Henderson Field from warships and sent troops ashore. A series of battles followed. On October 26, in the Battle of Santa Cruz off Guadalcanal between U.S. and Japanese warships resulted in the loss of the carrier *Hornet*.

Fighting on Guadalcanal raged. On November 14–15, the U.S. and Japanese warships clashed off Guadalcanal, resulting in the sinking of the U.S. cruiser *Juneau* and the deaths of the five Sullivan brothers.

A significant technological breakthrough occurred on December 2. Enrico Fermi conducted the world's first nuclear chain reaction test at the University of Chicago. This was opening of the door to the creation of an atomic bomb.

In the China Burma India Theater of operations, the Japanese were successful in attacking Calcutta, India, just before Christmas.

The year ended with Emperor Hirohito of Japan giving permission to his troops to withdraw from Guadalcanal after five months of bloody fighting against U.S. Forces.

★ ★ ★ ★ ★

In January 1943, the Casablanca Conference began. This was a meeting between U.S. president Franklin D. Roosevelt and his top military officers and Winston Churchill and his top military officers. The top military for FDR were General Arnold (USAAF), Admiral King (U.S. Navy), and General Marshall (U.S. Army). My cousin Dolly worked in Admiral King's office in Washington, DC. The doctrine of unconditional surrender was probably the most important agenda item discussed.[96]

The Battle of Stalingrad raged until February 2, 1943. The city was destroyed, but so was the German Sixth Army.[97]

Stalingrad turned into Germany's first major defeat in 1943, and the North Africa stalemate ended, with the surrender of the Axis powers to the Allies in Tunisia. The tide was finally turning.

JEFFERSON BARRACKS – 2/26/1943

During World War II, Jefferson Barracks was a major reception center for U.S. troops being inducted into the military. It also served as an important basic training site for the army and then later was the first Army Air Corps training site. The facility covered about 1,518 acres and had billeting space for 16 officers and 1,500 enlisted personnel. Jefferson Barracks was decommissioned as a military post in 1946 with the end of World War II.

I reported to Jefferson Barracks on February 26, 1943 for basic military training. It lasted about six weeks. It was a REALLY cold six weeks! While we were there, we were trained in basic military protocol: marching, discipline, courtesy, proper wearing of the uniform, and digesting army chow.

We stayed in little four-sided shacks. The sides were just four slabs of wood from the lumberyard. The slabs, with the bark still on them, were nailed to a frame. A large rope was tied around the shack to make sure it would stay together. Each shack could hold about eight men with just enough room for a coal-fueled heating stove in the center. There was a small pail of water next the stove to keep moisture in the air. We'd get the stove going, and it would get quite warm, so we'd throw our blankets off. There were supposed to be men going around during the night to restock the stoves, but that only occurred randomly. Occasionally, it would snow during the night. When it snowed, the snow would blow in through the cracks between the slabs. We would have a very rude awakening to one-fourth to one-half inch of snow on top of our blankets and a pail of frozen water. It felt like we were sleeping in a freezer!

Our days started early. Reveille was at 5:00 a.m. We'd do the standard military set of exercises, and then it was off to the chow hall. After breakfast, we spent the rest of the day learning how to be a soldier. After a month and a half of this routine, we were assigned to a CTD—College Training Detachment. My CTD was located at the Michigan State University campus in East Lansing. It was a relief to be leaving the "barracks" because spinal meningitis, colds, and the flu were prevalent throughout the camp. The one good thing I have to say about my experiences at Jefferson Barracks is that at the BX (base exchange), a pint of ice cream cost only 25 cents. I splurged every night!

Just as we were getting ready to leave Jefferson Barracks for Michigan State, there was a widespread outbreak of spinal meningitis at the barracks. So at the train station, they made everyone line up on a warehouse track. Then they shoved a thermometer in our mouth. Anyone who had a temperature of 102 or more got pulled aside. So of course, the guys in the line were sucking on the thermometer so it wouldn't read higher than about 100 degrees. There were between

1,000 and 1,500 of us who were allowed to board the train and depart Jefferson Barracks for Michigan State.

★ ★ ★ ★ ★

Fog of War: In China, General Chennault's Flying Tigers became the Fourteenth Air Force. That happened in March 1943. It would directly affect me later.

★ ★ ★ ★ ★

WAR IN EUROPE IN MARCH 1943

A total of 27 merchant vessels were sunk by Germany in the Atlantic in just four days. Thanks to codebreakers and long-range aircraft, serious losses were inflicted on the U-boats. Without their U-boats, Germany was no longer a threat in the Battle of the Atlantic.

**CTD – COLLEGE TRAINING DETACHMENT – 4/15/1943

CTD was a special program brought about by a shortage of flight school candidates. Initially, the Army Air Corps was only interested in selecting flight crew candidates from seniors at colleges. After graduation, these enlistees were sent to primary preflight school. This served as an orientation to the military and further screening for flight school. From there, they went into primary flight school. The Army Air Corps didn't feel these people needed more general education; they had already gotten what they needed at college. By the time I enlisted, the recruiters had run out of graduates and were willing to take anyone with any amount of college. These undergraduate recruits, like myself, then received additional classes at Michigan State through the CTD.

We went to school for five months, six days a week, eight hours a day. During that time, we received courses in physics, chemistry, and math. We ate in dining halls, not mess halls, and had nice, clean, warm quarters in the dormitories. The atmosphere was 180 degrees from that at Jefferson Barracks.

Upon graduation, we were awarded the equivalent of two full years of college. This qualified us to become a second lieutenant or a flight officer, similar to a warrant officer. In the final weeks of the CTD, we received about ten hours of orientations flights in small general aviation aircraft like Taylorcrafts and Piper Cubs. My instructor was a woman who had earned her instructor rating in 1932. She was an excellent instructor.

My graduating class at Michigan State numbered about 2,000 cadets/students, about 1,500 from Jefferson Barracks plus another 500 from a basic training base down in Miami, Florida. Most of us were under twenty years old.

The next stage of our training involved boarding a train and traveling to San Antonio, Texas. Our new home would be the San Antonio Aviation Cadet Center or SAACC, today known as Lackland AFB, part of Joint Force San Antonio.[1]

★ ★ ★ ★ ★

FOG OF WEAR

In May 1943, while I was still in CTD, the Fourteenth Air Force had acquired B-24 heavy bombers to conduct massive attacks against Japanese shipping along China's southeastern coast. I was unaware of this event, but it would have a significant effect on me when I finally finished training and received an assignment.

★ ★ ★ ★ ★

CHAPTER 5

Becoming a Pilot during Wartime

SACC – 9/1/1943

A T SACC, ON one side of the road, they had an area
for "classification," and on the other side was "preflight
for pilots." Everyone initially went through the "classification,"
where they took all kinds of tests: physical, psychomotor, mental,
psychological, etc. The most unusual test was the psychomotor. It
tested your coordination and how well your brain and other physical
parts (hands, feet, etc.) worked together, especially under stress.

Ultimately, everyone received a classification for particular jobs. The brightest ones were classified as navigators. From SAACC, the navigators went to San Marcos, Texas, for further training. Then were the pilots and bombardiers. Bombardiers went to Childress, Texas. Pilots just went across the street to preflight school. If you didn't qualify in those areas, you were further differentiated into aircraft engineers, radio operators, gunners, etc.

After the classification phase, I was classified as a pilot candidate. So I went across the street to preflight.

PREFLIGHT SCHOOL – 9/9/1943–11/12/1943

Preflight school was another three months of academics. There was more mathematics and physics, but they also included aircraft identification and Morse Code.

Aircraft identification was extremely important. If you are in a high-threat situation, one in which there are enemy aircraft wanting to shoot you down, you need to be able to tell the good guys from the bad guys. Basically, you would sit in a group or a team of two or three, and one of you would flip flash cards with a picture of an airplane on it, and the others would try to quickly identify it. As quickly as you identify one, that card is placed down, and another one is flipped up. The flash cards contained pictures of good guys as well as bad guys.

The longer you played the game, the less time you were allowed to identify the aircraft on the card. Also, the farther back the "flipper" would stand with the card, the smaller the image became. The time to identify a friend or foe was critical to survival. There's a saying among pilots, "First sight, first blood." You can't start shooting until you know who or what you are shooting at.

So to make the importance of this exercise even more clear, let's assume you're cruising along at 15,000 feet, looking into a clear blue sky. You, a heavy bomber, are moving toward the unknown aircraft at 250 mph. The other aircraft, a fighter, is approaching you at 350 mph.

If you are approaching each other nose to nose, your closure speed, the speed at which you are getting close to each other, is 600 mph!

The human eye can distinguish an object four feet wide, like the width of the fuselage of a fighter, at about 2 miles. At a closure speed of 600 mph, the fighter will be on you within twelve seconds of the time you spot him at two miles! However, you are twice or more the size of the fighter, so he has already seen you thirty seconds earlier.

While you are still looking for him, he's already planning his attack on you. So you have twelve seconds to find the fighter, visually identify it as a friend or foe, and identify its position for the formation.

As a bomber in a tactical formation, your mission is to put bombs on an assigned target. The gunners are the defense that you have. The pilot has to hold course, and the copilot has to be a second set of eyes for the gunners to identify unengaged threats. It all happens very quickly.

If you have an "angle off," that is, you and the fighter are not approaching head–on, you have a chance of seeing him sooner because you will be able to see some portion of the fuselage in addition to the front of the airplane. This will allow you a few more seconds to prepare for battle.

At the end of the course, there was a final exam. I was not too sharp in mathematics, so I didn't do as well as I had hoped. The lieutenant in charge called me in and said, "You know, Drumm, you didn't do too well in mathematics, so we don't know if we are going to be able to send you on to primary flight training." So I asked him, "What was my score?" He said, "Well, 70 was passing." I said, "But what did I get?" He said, "Well, you got 69.5. Do you think you ought to go?" I said, "Yes, sir!" He said, "Why?" I said, "Well, 69.5 rounded is considered 70!" He said, "Okay, Drumm, you're going. Now get out of here!"

So I left quickly before he could change his mind!

Fog of War: While I had been at BMT and CTD and SAAC, the war went on without me. Here's what happened while I was at CTD that would directly affect me later.

The War in Europe in 1943

In the Fall of 1943, Italy fell to Allied forces, prompting Germany to invade there. The Germans successfully rescued Mussolini and dominated in Northern Italy.

By the end of the year, the Soviets had the Germans retreating from Russia. The momentum in Europe looked as if it may have changed to the Allies.

The War in the Pacific in 1943

In the Pacific, Allied forces gained territory in New Guinea to attempt to protect Australia and Guadalcanal from Japanese invasion.

The high command in Japan had sent reinforcements to New Guinea in January and February. The convoy was made up of eight troop ships and eight destroyers. They were transporting seven thousand troops, aircraft fuel, and other supplies. A fighter escort of over one hundred planes was flying cover.

On March 1, 1943, U.S. reconnaissance aircraft saw and reported the convoy. Gen. George Kenny responded with 137 bombers and other fighter support aircraft to attack the convoy. The fighting lasted three days. All eight of the troop transports were destroyed, along with four of the destroyers. A total of 105 of the 150 Japanese fighters were destroyed. Over three thousand Japanese troops were killed or drowned, and all the supplies were sunk. A total of 213 tons of bombs had been dropped on the convoy by the American and Australian bombers.[98]

In April, U.S. codebreakers decoded a message that Admiral Isoroku Yamamoto, the master designer of the attack on Pearl Harbor, would be flying to from his headquarters in Rabaul to the Upper Solomons to inspect the Japanese bases there. The message included times, routing, and numbers and type of aircraft. There would be two "Betty" bombers, one carrying Yamamoto and the other carrying his staff. There would also be six "Zero" fighters flying escort.

The U.S. attack force consisted of sixteen P-38 "Lightning" fighters. Four would attack the two bombers, and the other twelve would dispatch the "Zero" escort. The intercept path was over one thousand miles long, and timing had to be perfect. It was. Unfortunately for Admiral Yamamoto, he was always punctual.

Three days later, several airmen from the Doolittle Raid were executed. This atrocity was followed by another one on May 14. A Japanese submarine sank the Australian hospital ship *Centaur*, resulting in 299 dead.

At the end of May, U.S. troops ended the occupation of the Aleutian Islands by the Japanese.

In June, the United States began submarine warfare against Japanese shipping, and the Allies advanced into New Georgia in the Solomon Islands.

The highlight in July was the bombing of the Japanese on Wake Island. The strike force was composed of B-24 Liberators flying from Midway.

On August 6–7, 1943, the Battle of Vella Gulf was fought in the Solomon Islands, and the Allied occupation of New Georgia was completed on August 25.

On September 4, Lae-Salamaua, New Guinea, was recaptured by the Allies.

At the beginning of October, the Japanese executed approximately one hundred American POWs on Wake Island. By the end of October, Emperor Hirohito realized that his country's situation is now "truly grave."

In November 1943, the two major objectives were driving the Japanese from the Solomon Islands and the Gilbert Islands. The actions taken included an invasion of Bougainville in the Solomon Islands by U.S. Marines. In the Gilbert Islands, Makin was invaded by the U.S. Army, and Tarawa was invaded by the U.S. Marines. The Japanese ended their resistance in Makin and Tarawa.

The Allied offensive continued in December with U.S. troops landing on the Arawe Peninsula of New Britain in the Solomon

Islands and a full Allied assault on New Britain as First Division Marines invaded Cape Gloucester, territory of New Guinea.

Primary Flight Training – 11/22/1943–1/28/1944

Primary flight training was at Victory Field in Vernon, Texas. The field was constructed as part of the Army Air Corps buildup for World War II. It was built and activated in 1941. It was assigned to the Air Corps Flying Training Command, Gulf Coast Training Center (later Central Flying Training Command).

The facility was a primary (stage 1) pilot training airfield operated under contract by Hunter Flying Service & Richey Flying Service. The flight instructors, aircraft maintenance, and housekeeping personnel were all civilians, but the detachment cadre were military. The commander of the school was an army major. We had nice brick quarters, a dining hall, and other facilities.

Fairchild PT-19 was the primary trainer at the airfield. It was a monoplane tail dragger, with a Ranger engine and two open cockpits in tandem (one behind the other). There was no radio in the aircraft.

Thousands of cadets were trained and made their first solo flight at Victory Field. As the war in Europe was drawing to an end, the need for pilot training was reduced. The army scheduled closed Victory Field in 1945.

My model of the PT-19 Trainer

USAF PT-19 Trainer

JERRY L. BURTON

Victory Field, Texas

We traveled there by train. Upon arrival, we were assigned a class number. Each class was given a designation reflecting the anticipated graduation year and the ID (A, B, C, etc.) of the group the trainee was in. My class was 44-F.

There were four of us in our flight. We got approximately sixty hours, and we were there for three months. All the sixty hours were in the PT-19.

During my time at primary, I reflected on what had happened to me and many young men like me. The Army Air Corps was enlisting kids right off the plow and the farm or just after graduating from high school. These kids were put into basic training and the CTD and then right into primary flight training in an airplane they had never seen before. Many of them didn't even know what an airplane was. But the Army Air Corps was sure they could train these young boys to fly.

As it turned out, it was a good program. The school focused on some ground school and the basic things about flying, like takeoffs and landings and how to do them safely. There were some other aerial maneuvers introduced such as stalls, slow rolls, loops, and things like that.

The PT-19 was an open-cockpit aircraft and was very noisy. You sat right behind the roaring engine, and then you had the air rushing by you like rapids in a river! Part of your equipment was a helmet with two gosports (earpieces) that protruded from each side of the helmet.

There was a rubber hose that came off each ear. The two hoses joined at a "Y," which joined in a single hose in back of you. The hose then went under the instructor's instrument panel and came up in front. On the instructor's end of the hose, he had a funnel that looked like a relief tube in a C-47. To communicate with the student, the instructor had to pull the throttle back, yell directions through the funnel, and then push the throttle forward again. Then he had to hope that the student heard, understood, and complied.

Victory Field had a paved runway, but we weren't allowed to use it. All our takeoffs and landings occurred from a large open pasture.

The most dangerous part of the training might have been each day at lunchtime. The air traffic was a zoo! Everyone was trying to come back and land at the same time. It really was amazing that there were no collisions. But everyone followed the prescribed procedure: forty-five-degree entry to the downwind, spacing on downwind, base, and final, touch down, slow down, and get off the field. These are the same procedures still used at un-towered fields today.

Despite the potential chaos, we had no fatalities. However, in my flight, we had two memorable "incidents."

★ ★ ★ ★ ★

BUCKLE UP

There were some strange and funny things that happened during the training. I remember one particular day when we showed up at the flight line. The instructor said, "Okay, guys, this morning I'm going to teach you how to do a slow roll. So this is how you do it." He demonstrated the maneuver by using his hands and a little model airplane. Throughout the demonstration, he asked us, "Do you have any questions?"

There was one little fellow among us; let's call him Frank. He couldn't have been more than about 5'2". Oh man! That guy was eager! He couldn't wait to get into that airplane and fly! He was just crazy about it! And so the instructor said, "Okay, Frank, you'll go first. Go ahead and preflight the airplane, and I'll be right out." So he did, and the instructor came out and said, "Frank, you ready to go?" And Frank said, "Oh yeah! Ready to go!" So the instructor told him to "Jump in and let's go."

So they were chugging along at about three to four thousand feet AGL, and the instructor said, "Now, Frank, you remember what I told you?" And Frank nodded. "Yes, sir, I remember. Oh yes." So the instructor said, "Well, first of all, I'm going to demonstrate one slow roll, and then after I have demonstrated it, you go ahead and try one." And Frank went, "Oh yeah!" The instructor then said, "You ready to go?" And Frank said, "Oh yeah. Let's do it!"

The PT-19 is not like today's jet aircraft where you can pick a point and roll on a point. It didn't have that much power. So you had to dive downward, come back up, and roll it upside down on your back and then continue on around to level. So the instructor dove the aircraft downward, brought her up, and rolled it on its back. Lo and behold, Frank fell out of the airplane!

So when the instructor got back to the field, we said, "Hey, where's Frank?" "Oh," he replied, "he fell out of the airplane." We said, "Where'd he fall out?" The instructor replied, "Oh, about ten miles out there." "Well, is he okay?" "Well, yeah. He popped his chute. He's all right." "Well, aren't you going to send a truck to pick him up? That parachute is heavy! Frank is just a little guy." "Hell no! Let him walk. That'll teach him next time to fasten his safety belt!" Frank did eventually get back. I guess he thumbed a ride back to Vernon.

★ ★ ★ ★ ★

FLYING HURDLE STAGES

We also had one other guy, Jim, or something like that. We had what we called hurdle stages. Two stanchions were set up across from each other, and a string was tied between them. Then you tied some rags to it so you could see it better. The string was about fifteen feet in the air. The object was to come down with the airplane just over the string without breaking it. Then there were two white lines. One was close to the stanchions, say about twenty-five feet, and then the other was about seventy-five feet farther down. The idea is that you were supposed to come in over the string and land between the two white lines.

So Jim came in about thirty feet over the string. He was way too high to glide to a landing between the two white lines. So he did something his instructor had demonstrated once for him. The maneuver was called a rudder control stall (similar to a "falling leaf"). He was still about twenty feet in the air when he just pulled back on the stick, stalled the airplane, and started doing rudder control stalls. One wing would drop, and Jim would push full opposite rudder, which would lift the fallen wing up with opposite rudder, but then the other wing would fall. Jim would then lift that low wing by applying full rudder on the opposite side to lift that wing. All the while, the aircraft is continuing to lose altitude—rapidly!

Finally, the airplane hit the ground. SQUISH! The gear went one way, and the airplane went another. When all the parts quit moving, old Jim just sat there in the airplane with a look on his face as if to say "Now what do I do?"

★ ★ ★ ★ ★

JERRY L. BURTON

Fog of War: The end of the year, November 28–December 1, 1943, saw Pres. Franklin Roosevelt, Winston Churchill, and Josef Stalin meeting in Iran to discuss the invasion of France. Fleet Admiral Ernest King was also in attendance. This information was, of course, classified and not made available in general.

OPERATION MATTERHORN

After Pearl Harbor, President Roosevelt put a high priority on attacking the Japanese mainland. At that time, the United States had no land-based aircraft that could fly a round-trip bombing mission against Japan. The B-29 program was under way, but the first production aircraft was still two and a half years away. It didn't roll out until February 1944.

So President Roosevelt instituted a plan called Operation Matterhorn. The plan was top secret and involved the use of bases, some not yet built, in China for launching B-29 attacks against Japan.

There were islands near Japan with air fields from which B-17 and B-24 bombers could reach Japan. However, these had all fallen into Japanese hands. The Allies had agreed that the war in Europe had to be won before England or France would help in the Pacific. Russia had signed a nonaggression pact with Japan, so they were not going to provide help.

★ ★ ★ ★ ★

CHAPTER 6

Basic and Advanced Flight Training

BASIC FLIGHT TRAINING – 2/14/1944–4/14/1944

AFTER COMPLETING PRIMARY flight school, we went by train to basic flight training at Enid AFB, OK (now Vance AFB). We arrived there in February 1944.

This base was all military: there were no civilian components. Most of the instructors were second and first lieutenants who were disgruntled because they had been assigned to an instructor position instead of being sent off to a war zone, where they could fulfill their dreams of bombing enemy targets or shooting down German or Japanese fighters in aerial combat. Unfortunately, they took it out on the students.

The program there was about sixty hours, same as primary flight school, but it was broken into two different phases. The first phase was the transition phase, where you learned to fly the BT-13 Valiant—or as we affectionately called it, the BT-13 Vibrator. Once in a while, without warning, the aircraft would vibrate—sometimes the prop would actually come off in flight.

Bill's model of the basic trainer, BT-13

Basic trainer, BT-13

The maneuvers we flew a basic flight school were the same as those we learned at primary. The difference was that we were relearning them in this heavier aircraft with its higher horsepower and canopy. We also learned how to use a two-way radio with intercom and how to fly in formation. The best part of all this for the instructor was that he could chew you out over the radio instead of having to yell over the prop noise.

One of the most apparent differences between primary and basic flight school was the runway. At primary, there was a runway, but we were not allowed to use it. We had to land in a vacant field.

Around noon, lunchtime, everybody came back at once, of course. We had no control tower to sequence the landing airplanes. But there was a procedure that we were to follow. That procedure was exactly the same as the noncontrolled airport procedures we use today. Amazingly, everyone was very good at executing the forty-five-degree entry leg to the pattern, flying a downwind, and turning base so as to allow proper spacing on final.

Having runways and radios in basic training was a tremendous improvement to the training program.

After achieving basic proficiency in the heavier airplane, we entered the instrument phase of training. In this phase, we learned only the basics of instrument flight. For instrument training in the actual airplane, there was a hood (like a curtain) that you could pull up over your head so you could see your instruments but not anything outside the airplane. If you did something wrong, the instructor would beat on your knees with the control stick! The sticks in both cockpits moved simultaneously.

A good friend of mine was flying with an instructor after we came back from Christmas. While in flight, the instructor, without warning, grabbed the stick and started "knee-beating" my friend for something my friend had done wrong. In the process of banging the stick back and forth and from side to side, the instructor smashed the new watch my friend had received as a present at Christmas! In addition to being a "knee beater," the instructor acted as "safety pilot" and watched outside for other aircraft and obstructions.

We also received ground instrument training in a simulator called a link trainer.

Link Trainer

The link trainer was a lot like climbing into a black coffin. It actually banked and pitched a few degrees for a sense of reality. There was a monitor who stood or sat outside the box and issued headings and other instructions to the student who was inside, with the overhead closure down and the instruments dimly lit. The monitor had a duplicate set of instruments on which he or she could monitor the student's responses.

We also spent a lot of time honing our cross-country and navigational skills. These became more important as we shifted focus to night flying. There was an auxiliary field[2] about thirty miles from our field. We'd go over there, and they'd stack us about five hundred feet apart on each end of the runway. As two aircraft completed their night takeoffs and landings, they would leave, and two more would take their place in the pattern. There was an instructor in an aircraft on the ground who would use his radio to control the entire activity.

So I remember this one night, I had finished my night requirements, and the instructor released me and another aircraft to go back to our home field. About seven or eight miles from the field, I called in and requested landing instructions. I got no answer. So I called in again—no answer. Again, I requested landing instructions—still, no answer after the third time. I was getting closer and closer, and I finally got a call that said, "This is the tower. Land on the highway east of the field." I said, "The what?" And I thought, *Land on the highway? That doesn't really make too much sense.* So instead, I climbed to about seven thousand feet and flew right over the top of the field and called in again. They told me which runway was active, so I came on in and landed.

Another guy who was cleared to land at the same time I was had landed and parked near me. We shut down our aircraft, secured them, and walked back carrying our parachutes to the operations shack. I told this fellow about my experience, and he said, "Oh, I heard you calling, and nobody would answer you, so I gave you those instructions!" What a jokester this guy was!

We finally finished our basic training in the BT-13 without anybody getting killed, although there were a couple of hair-raising experiences.

One source of excitement with the BT-13 involved a maximum allowable RPM of 2,700. If you exceeded 2,700 RPM, you were supposed to write it up in the logbook. Most of the guys did, but some didn't because when you exceeded the maximum RPM, you'd get your ass chewed. The reason for writing it up was that when 2,700 RPM was exceeded, the propeller would "crystallize" on the shaft and eventually come off.

We had two incidences of propeller loss. In one, the instructor pilot was sitting in the back with the student in front as they were taking off. They got about twenty feet in the air, and all of a sudden, BLING! There went the prop running down the runway. The instructor pilot grabbed the stick and did a rudder-controlled stall back down onto the runway. Fortunately, he was able to land the propeller-less aircraft safely.

The second incident occurred as one of the guys in my flight was cruising along at about seven thousand feet. All of a sudden, BLING! There went his prop! He had to do an emergency landing in a wheat field. Again, no one was injured.

Well, that was about the extent of the excitement—no deaths and a few screwy things and some minor injuries along the way.

One last comment about the flight instructors at basic. Most of them were excellent. However, I had one who didn't fit the mold. Frankly, I just couldn't tolerate him. I had twelve hours of dual in the BT-13, and he hadn't soloed me yet. So I went to the squadron commander and explained the situation to him. He assigned me to another instructor. After one hour of dual with the other instructor, he soloed me.

After our three months at Enid, some of us were off to single-engine advanced training in the AT-6, and others left for twin-engine training. I chose to go to twin-engine advance training.

So it was back on the train again, and off we went to Blackland Army Airfield in Waco, Texas.

★ ★ ★ ★ ★

Fog of War: In early February, the first B-29 rolled off the production line. Then in early April, B-29s began arriving in India. On April 24, 1944, the same day I began advanced flight training, the B-29s in India started making flights over the Hump into China with materials to support operations from bases in China. Again, the requirement for secrecy greatly reduced the circulation of this information.

★ ★ ★ ★ ★

Advanced Flight Training – 4/24/1944–6/27/1944

Finally, we were ready for advanced flight training (AFT)! The aircraft would be larger, heavier, and more complex than the relatively small, light single-engine trainers we had been flying. The fact that we now would have two engines to manage would change our workload and aircraft performance significantly. So having learned all the basic principles of flying, we were challenged with the prospect of applying all those principles to a different "platform."

The city of Waco had just begun construction of a municipal airport in the spring of 1942. Then on June 2, 1942, the army, needing fields for training pilots and aircrew, leased the site and finished construction of the runways and other facilities. The first name of the field was the China Spring Army Airfield. Then it became Waco Army Air Field #2. Later, it was redesignated Blackland Army Airfield.

Blackland Army Airfield in Texas served both as an Army Air Force advanced flight training field and a commercial civilian field for the city of Waco. We heard that when the commercial carriers landed, they pulled down the shades on the windows so passengers could not take pictures of the military operation across the field.

Discipline was pretty tight among the cadets in advanced training. Failure to comply with standards, like the military way to make a bed, could earn you a "tour." A tour was an hour of walking on the ramp (aircraft parking area) at attention with a parachute hanging from your rear end. Tours could also be "earned" by accumulating a certain number of demerits for "minor" infractions. The ramp could get very hot and humid during the months of May and June.

Blackland Tower and AT-17   AT-17s in formation flight

At Blackland, we trained in the AT-17, a twin-engine tail dragger. The engines were large radial engines. It had retractable landing gear and side-by-side seating as opposed to tandem, which was common in single-engine trainers. The first obvious challenge was flying an airplane with two engines. The second big challenge was flying an airplane with two engines when one of the engines wasn't running. The loss of one engine causes the airplane to move forward on the side with the good engine and to drag behind on the side with the "failed" engine. To compensate for the drag on the "dead" engine side of the airplane, you must push very hard on the rudder on the "good" engine side of the airplane. Your leg can get real tired real fast!

The other flying characteristics of the twin were very similar to single engine. The transition to the AT-17 was made enjoyable by the attitude of the instructors. They were far more "human" than the tigers at basic. They had the same rank but appeared to be more mature.

Formation flight in the AT-17 was just a matter of adjusting your reference points, so that was no problem. The navigation part of the program included something new—night cross-country. My instructor was very tolerant and patient. He helped me a lot in this phase of the training.

Advanced training went smoothly with few "stories" to tell. However, one flight was particularly memorable.

The AT-17 had an electrical system for lights, gear, etc. Maintenance had worked on one of the aircraft the night before this fateful flight. The next morning, two students took off in the airplane. Standard procedure is that you leave the gear down until there is no usable runway left. Then you bring the gear up. (Usable runway is defined as enough runway to put the airplane back down on the runway and brake to a safe stop.) The students had started their climb, so they hit the switch to bring the gear up. Instead of the gear coming up, both engines shut down! There is a big lake, Lake Waco, at the end of the runway. SPLASH!

They were pulled out of the lake and were okay—just wet!

So we finally came to the end of our training. I graduated on June 27, 1944, as a flight officer (F/O). We were now full-fledged pilots in the Army Air Corps!

Congress only authorizes so many commissions, even in wartime. The army was churning out more pilots than there were authorized commissions. Prior to World War II, they had enlisted pilots, but that program had been cut. For the enlisted pilots, they created a rank called the flight officer. The flight officer got the same pay as a second lieutenant. The only difference was that the flight officer wore a blue bar like a warrant officer. Also, instead of the spread eagle on his cap, he wore a "ruptured duck."

I came out as a flight officer, not a second lieutenant. (I was in good company though. Chuck Yeager, the famous test pilot, also graduated as a flight officer.) Either way, the wings were the same!

★ ★ ★ ★ ★

Fog of War: On June 5, 1944, the B-29s began flying missions from India. Their targets were in Burma and China.

On June 6, 1944, the Allies launched their attack on the beaches of Normandy. The Battle of Normandy, often referred to as D-Day, lasted from June 1944 to August 1944 and resulted in the liberation of Western Europe from Nazi Germany's control.

The Battle of the Philippine Sea, also known as the Great Marianas Turkey Shoot, occurred on June 19–20, 1944. It was the last "carrier" battle of the war and resulted in the annihilation of Japan's naval aviation. It also opened the door for the use of the Marianas and Guam for B-29 bases.[99]

The need for secrecy also veiled these operations.

★ ★ ★ ★ ★

CHARTER 7

Fighters, Bombers, or Cargo
Where to from Here?

TOWARD THE END of advanced flight school, our instructor asked us what kind of combat aircraft we would like to go into that had more than one engine. I told him my first choice was the Lockheed P-38. He said, "It's only fighter pilots who go into P-38s." So I said, "Well, how about a B-26, you know, the one with the cigar-shaped fuselage?" "Oh," he said, "you're too far down the list for that. How about a B-24?" "A what?" I replied. "What's a B-24? I never heard of it." He said, "Well, it's a four-engine bomber with twin tails." It sounded like a challenge, so I said, "Well, all right, let's try it."

So I received orders for transition training in the B-24. Off I went to Liberal, Kansas. My girlfriend, Mary Lou, lived in Kansas City. I contacted her, and she met me at the train station. We were able to visit for an hour before I reboarded and continued to Liberal. While we were visiting, I was approached by the military police. They had an issue with my uniform. As a flight officer, the emblem on my hat should have been the "ruptured duck." Instead, I had mistakenly used the "spread eagle," which was authorized only for commissioned officers.

SPREADEAGLE (photo courtesy of USAMM):   RUPTURED DUCK (photo courtesy of USAMM):

It was a small infraction but embarrassing nonetheless to be written up in front of my girlfriend. Then refaced, I boarded the train and continued my journey to Liberal.

★ ★ ★ ★ ★

Fog of War: Another top secret, limited distribution plan was quickly coming together. In early 1944, the Manhattan Project was front and center. Roosevelt had approved the Manhattan Project in January 1942. Now in mid–September 1944, the project was experiencing problems in achieving an adequate amount of enriched uranium to produce even one bomb. The two enrichment complexes at Oak Ridge, Tennessee, were using "pure" uranium as initial input to the enrichment process in their K-25 and Y-12 diffusers. Oak Ridge was the official enrichment operation and part of the Manhattan Project under Maj. Gen. Leslie Groves. The K-25 gaseous diffuser only slightly enriched the uranium. That slightly enriched uranium then served as input to the Y-12 gaseous diffuser. The output from the K-12 was still below weapons grade.

Roosevelt had declared that only the U.S. Army should play a role in the Manhattan Project. However, the U.S. Navy had been working at the Philadelphia Naval Yard on enriching uranium for a nuclear submarine. Another scientist, Philip Abelson, was using a thermal method of enrichment. Instead of using "pure" uranium as initial input, Abelson used UF_6, uranium hexafluoride. His thermal diffusion method of enrichment, S-50, provided a much higher level of enrichment than did the K-25 to Y-12 process.

Theoretical physicist J. Robert Oppenheimer sent a telegram to Groves suggesting that he should take a look at Abelson's process and results. Oppenheimer believed that if the three processes, K-25, Y-12, and S-50, were used together, weapons-grade enriched uranium could be produced.

Groves approved the plan, and construction on an S-50 plant was begun immediately at Oak Ridge. The contractors were given ninety days to complete the construction. They finished it in just sixty-nine days.[100]

★ ★ ★ ★ ★

Transition Training – B-24 – 7/10/1944–9/15/1944

After arriving in Liberal, I went through processing. I had assumed the uniform infraction in Kansas City was behind me. I was wrong. The infraction had made its way in writing and now appeared before me in the form of the administrative officer, a first lieutenant. He welcomed me with a warm chewing out!

JERRY L. BURTON

Liberal AAF was officially opened on May 13, 1943. It was placed under the jurisdiction of the Army Air Forces Pilot School (Specialized 4-Engines), II Bomber Command, Second Air Force. The mission of the base was to train Consolidated B-24 Liberator heavy bomber pilots, who were predominantly newly commissioned officers graduated from training command advanced twin-engine flying schools. George McGovern, later a senator and candidate for president of the United States, trained as a B-24 pilot at Liberal.

I had arrived at Liberal after dark. The next couple of days were spent in orientations. Finally, we were taken to the flight line and introduced to the B-24. My instructor had barely described what I saw in front of me! He left out the parts about the beast being huge, grossing at 58,000 pounds on takeoff, carrying a crew of ten, and that all the flight controls were manual—a real exercise machine!

I stood and stared at the aircraft. It just sat there, almost defiantly. I thought, *I'll never learn to get all that metal up in the air and down on the ground again in one piece. I had my hands full with 5,300 pounds and two engines!*

A B-24 "Liberator"—in the flesh!

This was not your typical trainer! Ten times heavier, two more engines, more instruments to watch, turbos, oxygen, and on and on. It seemed an impossible task to complete in three months.

But as with everything else, I went through the transition, learned how to fly the airplane, and then did instrument training, etc. Three months later, mission accomplished.

Not everyone in transition training was so lucky. One day Liberal had an open house for the public. I remember watching a B-24 practicing an instrument approach. He was about 250 feet above the ground as he turned onto final. The instructor pulled the power back on the two inside engines. This was a way to simulate engine failure. The "student" pilot applied power to the other two engines. The aircraft hit the ground and cartwheeled down the runway. I had AB+ blood type and was called on to donate blood for one of the survivors.

I was ready to go from Liberal to Lincoln, Nebraska, and pick up a B-24 crew and fly to Boise, Idaho, for combat crew training. That training teaches the whole crew to work together as a unit under combat conditions. But we were told there was not space for us at crew training. So we were held over for another month.

A friend, Edward Eddy (yes, Eddie Eddy), and I went to base ops to get four hours of flight time so we would qualify for flight pay. Ops had a BT-13 on the ramp. We had flown the BT-13 in basic training. What luck! This was going to be a piece of cake.

First thing that went wrong was that we couldn't start the darn thing. We had to ask the line chief how to start it. We got it started, taxied out to the active, and took off. We nearly killed ourselves on takeoff! The control pressures required to fly the BT-13 were a small fraction of the pressure we had become accustomed to horsing the B-24 around.

We knew by now that there was nothing exciting to do in Liberal, Kansas, so Eddie and I decided to go AWOL to Wichita.

The excitement of the "big" city wore off after about three days. We went over to the base in Wichita hoping to get a ride back to Liberal. Fortunately, two instructor plots were there and gave us a ride back. They also told us our orders had been cut for crew training.

When we got back, we expected to be questioned about where we had been. It was almost disappointing to find out that no one had missed us.

★ ★ ★ ★ ★

On July 20, 1944, there was a failed assassination attempt against Hitler. Then about a month later, on August 25, the Allies liberated Paris.

COMBAT CREW TRAINING – 9/18/1944–1/26/1945

CREW FORMATION

From Liberal, Kansas, we went to McCook Army Airfield in Lincoln, Nebraska, to pick up a B-24 combat crew.

McCook AAF was one of eleven U.S. Army Air Forces training bases in Nebraska during WWII. It was a major training site for celestial navigation, gunnery and bombing, and communications, radar, and aircraft maintenance. The base had been activated on April 1, 1943.

McCook provided final training of heavy bomber crews for the B-17 Flying Fortress, the Consolidated B-24 Liberator, and the Boeing B-29 Superfortress. Around fifteen thousand servicemen and five hundred civilians were stationed at McCook.

Well, I was supposed to pick up a crew: a copilot, navigator, bombardier, engineer, radio operator, ball gunner, nose gunner, tail gunner, and waist gunner. From there, my crew and I would have gone to Gowen AAF in Boise, Idaho. But at McCook, I was told by a staff sergeant that I didn't have enough rank to be the pilot of a B-24 with a crew, but I could go on as a copilot.

So I signed on to the crew of Bob Cox, a man I knew in advance flight training at Waco and Liberal. And finally, I was headed to Gowen as a copilot on Bob's crew.

My "First" Crew

Back row: F/O William Drumm, copilot, Indiana; F/O Harold Clouser, navigator, Pennsylvania; Lt. Robert Cox, pilot, Indiana

Front row: Cpl. Robert Wuertz, nose gunner, New Jersey; PFC Charles Willsey, tail gunner, Kansas; Cpl. Charles Niley, ball turret, South Carolina; Cpl. Norman Marks, waist gunner, California; Cpl. Willis Denny, radio operator, Ohio; Cpl. Bill Elias, flight engineer, Wisconsin

★ ★ ★ ★ ★

Within a month of arriving at Gowen, B-29s launched out of Saipan in the Marianas successfully struck Tokyo and returned to their base on Saipan. Thereafter, Tokyo was struck often by B-29s dropping firebombs.

★ ★ ★ ★ ★

CREW TRAINING

Gowen Field Gate House

Gowen AAF

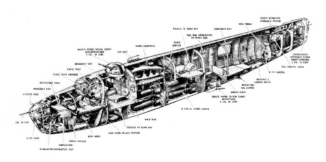

B-24J Cutaway

B-24D

A little more than halfway through September, we started our crew training at Gowen.

Crews always trained together but sometimes used a different aircraft, depending on aircraft operational status and scheduling. I trained with Bob Cox for only about two months.

About halfway through our training, I was told that some other flight officers and I were to meet a promotion board. If we passed, we would be commissioned second lieutenants. There were ten questions on the test, each one worth ten points. They must have been hard up for second lieutenants—we all got 100 percent on the test!

The squadron commander called us all in on Saturday after the test and told us that several crews had lost their pilots. We would be assigned to those crew and go through training again as command pilots.

It was around mid-November, and I had been through half the course as a copilot. Now I was going to restart crew training but this time as the pilot. The first thing I did was meet the other officers in my new crew for dinner. The next day, Sunday, I met with the enlisted members of my new crew. The following morning, Monday, we began our first training together at 0430.

Front row (L–R): George G. Ronnenkamp, engineer; John C. Baldwin, radio operator; Grady B. Yawn, nose gunner; James E. Kincheloe, ball gunner; James T. Pleak, waist gunner; Sidney Bergman, tail gunner

Back row (L–R): William H. Drumm, pilot; Thomas J. Massey, copilot; George D. Iseminger, navigator; Robert V. Bertram, bombardier

We went through crew training at Gowen Field, Boise, Idaho, from December 1944 to March 1945. We were the number 1 crew in our class at Gowen Field. Subsequently, we were assigned to the 14th Air Force, 308th Bomb Group, 375th Bomb Squadron in China and later to Rupsi, India, where they flew twenty-seven missions over the "Hump" before WWII ended. We were one of the last crews of the 375th Bomb Squadron to leave the China Burma India Theater of operations in the latter part of 1945.

★ ★ ★ ★ ★

At Gowen, we worked well together as a crew, and it was about halfway through the training program when we were notified that we were number 1 in crew competition! We were very pleased because the other crews were extremely competitive.

Unfortunately, one crew member showed up late for a mission one morning. That event and one other caused us to slip into fourth place among all the classes by the end of our training. However, all the men were excellent professionals at their positions. Two in particular, Engineer George Ronnenkamp and Navigator George Iseminger, were outstanding throughout the program.

Training at Gowen Field was a very new and unique experience. Everything prior to Gowen—basic military training, academics, flight training in primary, basic, advanced, and then transition in the B-24—was all in preparation for the final phase of training at Gowen. Here, ten men from all parts of the country, different walks of life, trained in their own specialties, were joined together to function as a crew, a team, as one unit among many weapons of war for WWII. Everyone had to understand what the others' specialty was, and each (pilots, engineers, navigators, gunners, bombardiers, radio operators) had to depend on the others to do their jobs well.

I feel that the training we received at Gowen and, in fact, all the training we received along the way was the best in the world. In fact, there was a sense of realism in everything we did. For example, gunnery training included P-38s running mock attacks on us. In addition, we had bombing practice on a target range. We practiced both day and night bombing.

There were, of course, glitches, and sometimes people screwed up. But in my class, from beginning to end, there were no fatalities. As I think back about these times, it occurs to me that all of us were between the ages of nineteen and twenty-seven. The military experience pulled the very best out of all of us!

★ ★ ★ ★ ★

JERRY L. BURTON

CHAPTER 8

Goings On at Gowen

STORIES

AS I WENT through the combat crew training, there were four events that I remember vividly. I'll share these "special" memories with you.

SAFETY FIRST

As a safety factor, I had briefed the crew that under no circumstances would anyone light up a cigarette until the flight engineer said it was okay to smoke. One morning as we took off, I smelled cigarette smoke. Just then, the flight engineer came up and told me that one of the gas caps on the left wing had come off, and we were siphoning fuel. Siphoning fuel and lit cigarettes could make for a very bad ending.

I remained in the pattern, came back around, and landed. Needless to say, I had a few choice words for the culprit—one of the officers. But it never happened again!

★ ★ ★ ★ ★

JACK FROST BITES

Winter can really get cold up in Idaho. I remember one January night when we flew a practice bombing mission. The entire crew had to go anytime we were practicing combat whether they had a direct role. We were at about fifteen thousand feet, and it was cold as ★★★★, forty-three degrees below zero. All the gunners and everybody were sitting in the back end. The heat wasn't working in the airplane.

Bob Bertram, the bombardier, was trying his best to put the bombs on target but with little success. His hands were just about frozen, and it was very difficult for him to do his job. Every run was the same. We'd start the run, and he'd say, "Okay, I've got the airplane." I would acknowledge, "Okay, you've got the airplane." He'd try to get down on the target, and then all of a sudden, he'd say, "Dry run." I'd moan and think, "Oh no. Not again!"

Those poor guys in the back! Every time Bob would announce "dry run," you could hear a loud groan go up in the back of the airplane. After about two hours, we finally got off the range and down to a lower altitude.

I'm probably not alone when I say that's one of my most memorable bomb runs!

★ ★ ★ ★ ★

A STROKE OF "BAD" LUCK

As part of our training, we had to fly some night cross-countries. One of those was a round trip to Las Vegas, Nevada, and back. When arrived in the Las Vegas area, as luck would have it, the flight engineer informed me that the number 3 engine was running too rich, and we had to land for gas and repairs. I couldn't object because, after all, it was a safety of flight issue. So we had to RON (remain overnight) and make repairs in the morning.

JERRY L. BURTON

It's just one of the many sacrifices you have to make! (Oh, we did notice that they were just putting up a new casino, the Flamingo, on the Strip.)

★ ★ ★ ★ ★

On October 12, 1944, about a month into the crew training, Tokyo had been bombed by B-29s from Saipan in the Marianas. It was the first land-based bombing of Tokyo in the war. The B-29s continued fire-bombing Tokyo and other cities in Japan. The psychological effect on the Japanese was incredible.

The Battle of Leyte Gulf, the largest naval battle of the war and possible of all time, began on October 23 and ended on October 26, 1944. It involved over two hundred thousand naval personnel. This victory by the U.S. Navy enabled the invasion of the Philippines.[101]

GET OUT OF HERE AND DON'T COME BACK!

Just before Christmas 1944, we were on the bombing range and doing some formation flying. We had just cleared the range and rejoined the formation when we noticed a huge cloud of dust from the ground up to about ten thousand feet rolling in from the northwest!

A call was made to Gowen Tower, advising them of the weather phenomenon and requesting landing instructions. The response was not what we expected. "Sorry, old boy, you can't land because we've got some inbound B-24s from Walla Walla, Washington. They're running low on fuel, so we've got to get them in first. You guys will have to divert to Wendover, Utah." "Wendover where?" I replied. "Where the heck is Wendover, Utah?" The navigator finally found it and said, "Hey, I found it. I know where it is!"

On the range with us were some other guys from Mountain Home, another B-24 crew training school. In all, we were a "fleet" of twenty-three B-24s. But as directed, we all headed to Wendover, Utah.

Wendover AAF

We landed, taxied in, shut down, and got out of the airplanes. All of a sudden, we were surrounded by troops with guns in six by six. They said, "Okay, you guys, just get in the truck and don't say anything!"

They took us to a holding area that was fenced in. It had a barracks, and I think a chapel, a theater, and a mess hall. Once inside the area, they said, "Now we want you to stay in this area, and if we find you outside this area, we're going to shoot you. No questions asked!" "What?" I thought, *Boy, you're the most inhospitable people we've ever seen.*

So we were there for three days before they came back around in their six-by-six. They put us back in the trucks and took us back to the airplanes. Then they told us, "Get into your airplanes and get out of here! We don't ever want to see you guys here again!" I thought, *Boy, are you guys unfriendly!*

We all took off and went to our respective bases, wondering what in the world we had dropped in on.

★ ★ ★ ★ ★

Fog of War: Most of the guys in crew training knew something about the new B-29. But when you're undergoing specific training for combat, your focus is on the missions you're training for and honing the skills of your crew as a unit. You don't have a lot of time

JERRY L. BURTON

for other things. What we didn't know was that an atomic bomb, whatever that was, was being developed. That information was far above what would ever be shared with us.

I assume that the range control people had given Wendover control a "heads-up" on the diversion of our flights. Twenty-three bombers approaching unannounced to a military field could get someone in a whole lot of trouble, even if there was nothing special going on there.

Three months earlier, in September 1944, the 393rd Bombardment Squadron had been moved to Wendover, Utah. Along with it went a large team of scientists and ordnance specialists responsible for "everything" about the atomic bomb as a weapon. This included modifications to the B-29 bomb bays and the mechanics of loading the bomb whose diameter exceeded the height from the ground to the bomb bay opening. The solution was a narrow pit. The "bomb" was lowered down into the pit. The B-29 was then pushed back over the pit, and the bomb was raised by a hydraulic jack up into the bomb bay and secured.

Unclassified Now
"Little Boy" in the pit

Unclassified Now

"Little Boy" ready to be loaded into the *Enola Gay*

Col. Paul W. Tibbets, the pilot who delivered the first atomic bomb, was the commander of the 509th. His mission was the oversite of the operation at Wendover but also involved him flying and dropping dummy "atomic bombs" to determine the optimum maneuvers for delivery.

From "outside the fence," the operation had the appearance of a "normal" military bomber training field and range. They had some B-24 stations there, along with a few fighter aircraft. Inside the fence was a different story. Wendover Field had been chosen because of its isolation and the need for absolute security.[102]

It would be a gross understatement to say that the arrival of Bill and his comrades at Wendover Field was poorly timed!

★ ★ ★ ★ ★

It wasn't until after the war, about 1954, they released a film with Robert Taylor (*Above and Beyond*), who was playing the part of Paul Tibbetts. It was Colonel Tibbets who flew the *Enola Gay* and dropped the bomb on Hiroshima.

That was the operation that we dropped in on and caused such a stir. No wonder they were so "nasty to us"—"Don't come back here!" None of us had any idea what was going on there!

In the 1960s, I was assigned to the Pentagon, and Paul Tibbets was director of management analysis at that time. I was in that directorate. He had been promoted to a general officer, so we didn't share the same professional or social circles. However, I did see him at one of our Flying Tigers get-togethers down in Texas.

As for keeping us under lock and key for three days, I now believe that they were running clearances on all our aircrews to confirm that there were no unauthorized persons or "spies" on any of the twenty-four aircraft we flew in on.

★ ★ ★ ★ ★

Fog of War, 1944: I had been in training schools during all of 1944 and the first month of 1945. So I missed most of what was going on in the outside world during that time.

THE WAR IN EUROPE IN 1944

The war in Europe had begun to shift back toward the Allies in 1944. France had been taken back from the Germans after the surprise landings in Normandy. Italy had been liberated. And the Soviets had pushed the Germans all the way back to Warsaw, Poland.

The one "hitch" was at the Battle of the Bulge, which had begun on December 16, 1944, and ended on January 25, 1945. Hitler had made some staff changes that implied to the Allies that Germany was assuming a defensive posture. However, that was part of a deception that allowed the Germans to assemble an incredibly large force of men, tanks, and artillery in the area of the Ardennes. At the same time, they had a more visible force assembling father north and directly across from the area chosen by the Allies for their "final" thrust into Germany.

Hitler's German forces attacked through the Ardennes with two hundred thousand men. They faced only eight thousand American soldiers. The German army also had around 1,000 tanks and 1,900 pieces of artillery. Their air forces numbered 2,000 aircraft, including some Messerschmitt Me 262 jets.

Fortunately for the Allies, there were other units nearby who could reinforce the Americans up by the Ardennes. The other fortunate thing for the Allies is that they had a good supply chain. The Germans, on the other hand, were short of fuel, ammunition, and food.

The Battle of the Bulge was among the most ferocious battles of the war. It was the last real offensive to be launched by the Germans.[103] With the loss of this battle, Germany was about to go down in defeat.

The War in the Pacific in 1944

In the Pacific, the Allies were gaining ground. Through the efforts of the British, their Indian forces, Merrill's Marauders, and General Wingate's attacks behind Japanese lines, much of Burma had been recaptured. Eventually, the Japanese started withdrawing forces from Burma and China in anticipation of an invasion of their homeland.

The U.S. Navy and their marines were winning back many of the Pacific islands, but it was at a very high cost in lives. Some of the well-known battles of the navy were the U.S. carrier-based strikes on Truk in the Caroline Islands, the air strikes on the Marianas, and the destruction of the Japanese base at Rabaul.

The Japanese made their last offensive in China in April 1944. They attacked the U.S. air bases in Eastern China. Again, after those attacks, the Japanese began pulling troops back toward their homeland. Also, in April and May, the Allies begin taking back more of New Guinea with the invasion of Aitape, Hollandia, and Biak. As you may remember, two years earlier, the Battle of the Coral Sea occurred off New Guinea.

A big game changer occurred in June. The first B-29 Superfortress bombers struck the Japanese railway facilities in Bangkok, Thailand. Thailand, by the way, was on the side of the Japanese.

The U.S. Marines continue to retake islands from the Japanese. These islands were important because either they had Japanese airfields on them that our bombers could use to attack Japan or they were suitable for the Seabees to construct airstrips for our bombers.

Another important event was the June bombing of the steel works at Yawata. This was the first raid on Japan since the Doolittle Raid of April 1942. The strike force consisted of forty-seven B-29s based in Bengal, India.

June was a big month for the newcomers, the B-29s. But the navy was scoring big too. In the Marianas, U.S. carrier-based fighters shot down 220 Japanese planes. American losses were only 20 airplanes. The air battle became known as the Marianas Turkey Shoot.

U.S. Marines continued their great work by invading Guam and Tinian. The Seabees began building a facility on Tinian that would later become the launching point for the B-29s carrying the atomic bombs to Hiroshima and Nagasaki.

In China, U.S. and Chinese troops took Myitkyina, in Burma, after a two-monthlong siege.

The noose tightened as the United States made air strikes against Okinawa. Fourteen B-29s, by this time based on the Marianas, attacked the Japanese base at Truk, and U.S. Sixth Army invaded Leyte in the Philippines. The Battle of Leyte Gulf resulted in a decisive U.S. Naval victory. During this battle, on October 25, 1944, the Japanese for the first time used suicide air (kamikaze) attacks against the U.S. warships. By the end of the war, Japan would have sent close to three thousand kamikazes against the Allies. The kamikazes did considerable damage sinking between thirty-five and sixty ships with a loss of approximately five thousand lives.[104]

The assumption at this time was that the Allies would have to invade the Japanese homeland to force a surrender. This required moving invasion forces as close as possible to Japan. It also meant destroying as much of the Japanese infrastructure and war-making capability as possible before an invasion. By this time in the war, Allied victory was assumed, but the cost in human lives would be extremely high. The atomic bomb was still nine months away from even being tested. Plan A was invasion.

On November 11, 1944, the U.S. Navy began bombardment of Iwo Jima in preparation for an invasion by U.S. Marines. It would be February 1945 before an invasion could be launched. Iwo Jima was part of a chain of small islands that served as an interior defense for the Japanese mainland. Iwo Jima was important to the Allies for two reasons. First, it would become important as a launch position for an invasion when the time came. Second, until an invasion could occur, the Seabees could improve the existing airfields so they could be used for emergency landing of B-29s as necessary. They would also be "home" for P-47 and P-51 fighters when Iwo was captured.

In November, twenty four B-29s bombed the Nakajima aircraft factory. That factory was located near Tokyo, so by this time, the Japanese were feeling somewhat desperate. The Japanese fleet of aircraft had been reduced considerably, and airpower had become a minor payer, at best.

On December 15, 1944, U.S. troops invaded Mindoro in the Philippines. This was a continuation of the invasion made possible by the Battle of Leyte Gulf in October.

To close out the year, on December 17, 1944, the U.S. Army Air Force began preparations for dropping the atomic bomb by establishing the 509th Composite Group in Westover, Utah. The small fleet of B-29s would develop the maneuver(s) required to accurately deliver the bomb. The unit had been there less than two weeks when Bill Drumm and the twenty-two other B-24s "dropped in" for their three-day visit.

★ ★ ★ ★ ★

As 1945 began, I was still in crew training at Gowen with one more month to go. During that month, this is what happened in the Pacific.

The British captured more area in Burma, and by the end of the month, the Burma Road was reopened. The U.S. Sixth Army began reoccupying the Philippines, and the U.S. Navy was dominating the seas enough to move into the Gulf of Thailand and the South China Sea and launch air raids into Indochina from their carriers.

The Japanese were back on their heels.

★ ★ ★ ★ ★

In CBI – Operation Matterhorn[105]

Operation Matterhorn kicked off in February 1944. The operation was dependent on airfields in India and China that had runways long enough and hard enough to handle the weight and takeoff distances required for the B-29 operations. It was an uphill battle, but the objective was met.

There were five airfields in the flatlands west of Calcutta that had 6,000-foot runways and enough area around them to extend their runways to at least 8,500 feet and support a weight of 70 tons. These airfields were located at Chakulia, Dudhkundi, Kharagpur, Piardoba, and Kalaikunda. Kalaikunda would serve as a transport base. The aircraft located at this base would be transporting fuel and equipment to the B-29 operations in China. At the same time the bases in India were being modified, the four "receiving" airfields in China were being constructed in the area around Chengtu. The plan called for airfields at Hsinching (A-1), Kwanghan (A-3), Kuinglai (A-5), and Pengshan (A-7). These airfields would serve as the forward bases for the B-29s that would strike Japan. The B-29s located in India would strike Japanese strongholds in China and Manchuria.

The lengthening of the runways of the bases in India was going slowly. To enhance the probability of having these five bases ready in time for planned operations, another base, at Charra, had its 6,000-foot runway extended by using mats. Charra had been a B-24 Liberator airfield and was only used temporarily for the B-29s.

The first B-29s arrived in India in April and May 1944. They began flying transport missions to the airfields in China. Some strike missions were flown from the airfields in India against targets in Manchuria and in China.

The Himalayas are the highest, most treacherous mountains in the world, and the B-29 was not yet the world's most efficient aircraft. Flying fuel, ammunition, bombs, parts, and supplies over "the Hump" from India to China and back required six B-29 logistics flights to make possible just one B-29 bombing mission against Japan.[106]

There were no raids on Japan from India or China on missions flown after January 17, 1945.[107]

In February, the XX Bomber Command began withdrawing its units from CBI and moving them to the Marianas. By May 1945, the last of the B-29s were out of CBI.[108]

★ ★ ★ ★ ★

During World War II, hundreds of young men joined the Army Air Forces/Army Air Corps and trained to be pilots and crew members of the United States' bomber fleet.

Men from all parts of the country and different walks of life were trained in individual specialties such as pilots, copilots, navigators, bombardiers, engineers, gunners, and so forth. They were then joined together as crews and trained together. From there, they went to war.

My training was over. It was time to go to war.

★ ★ ★ ★ ★

JERRY L. BURTON

CHAPTER 9

Getting to "Over There"

WELL, WE FINALLY completed all our B-24 crew training. We were then sent to Santa Ana, California, to await further orders. Rumor had it we would be going to the Pacific.

Santa Ana Army Air Base had been built during the early part of World War II and was activated on January 1, 1942. It was used for basic training but had no planes, hangars, or runways. The base was located in Costa Mesa among Baker Street on the north, Harbor Blvd. on the west, Wilson Street on the south, and Newport Blvd. on the east.

With the activation of the base came the establishment of the West Coast Air Corps Training Center. The center commanded flying training (basic, primary, and advanced) at airfields in the Western United States. On July 31, 1943, it was redesignated as the Western Flying Training Command.

So we were at the Western Flying Training Command for a week or two. They gave us both summer and winter uniforms. Finally, they put us on a train and told us that our destination was secret. One car on the train served as a mess hall. The other cars were converted boxcars that served as sleeping quarters with bunks four high. Although the train made many stops, we weren't allowed off the train at any time—secret orders, you know. We ate and slept on the train for seven days.

I think we went through El Paso, up to Chicago, and then seven days later, we ended up, where else, New York City! But we still didn't know where we were going or what we would be doing.

We stayed in New York City (actually at Fort Totten) for about four days. It was my first time in the "Big Apple." Bob Bertram, the bombardier, and I went down to Times Square and to the theater to see the musical *Oklahoma!* Bob had a cousin in the show. We went backstage after the performance to meet her.

Next, we were put on a C-54 and flown from New York to the Azores.

C-54 military transport (USAAF photo)

NYC to Azores (Portugal)

Then we went to Africa (Casa Blanca).

Azores to Casablanca

I believe we RONd in Casablanca. I did not see Humphrey Bogart or Lauren Bacall in Casablanca; the club was closed the night that we were there.

Then we went across Africa to Cairo, Egypt.

Casablanca to Cairo

I believe we RONd in Cairo. The route was not direct. We had stops many places along the northern coast of Africa. It took several days to make the trip from Casablanca to Cairo.

Cairo to Oran to Algiers

Algiers to Tunis to Tripoli

Tripoli to Benghazi

Benghazi to Cairo

From Cairo, we flew to Abadan, Iran.

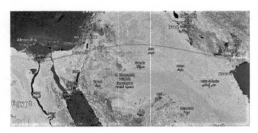

Cairo to Abadan, Iran

From Abadan, we flew to Karachi.

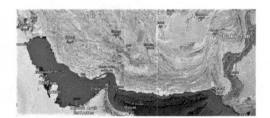

Abadan to Karachi

Finally, we flew into Pandaveswar.

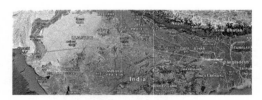

Karachi to Pandaveswar

JERRY L. BURTON

THE WAR IN EUROPE DURING THE FIRST THREE MONTHS OF 1945

Another Conference of Allied leaders, the Yalta Conference, occurred on February 4, 1945. Winston Churchill, Pres. Franklin D. Roosevelt, and Joseph Stalin were the Allied leaders. They were accompanied by their military leadership as well. Fleet Admiral King was there as the U.S. Naval leader.

Between 1942 and 1945, Pandaveswar (Pandabeswar) was a major combat airfield. The Tenth Air Force was the host unit. Known units there included the following:

4th Combat Cargo Group, C-46 Commandos, from November 1945 to January 15, 1946

7th Bombardment Group, B-24 Liberators, from December 12, 1942 to January 17, 1944

8th Photographic Reconnaissance Group, Nonflying, from January 3 to October 1943

12th Bombardment Group, B-25 Mitchell, from June 13 to July 16, 1944

427th Night Fighter Squadron, P-61 Black Widow, from October 31 to December 23, 1944

CHAPTER 10

Flying Tigers

P ANDAVESWAR ALSO SERVED as a staging area for the 308th Bomb Group, 14th Air Force stationed in China. There, my crew and I were assigned to Chennault's 14th AF as Flying Tigers. We were Flying Tigers until the war ended.

Chennault was funny—he didn't care for four-engine aircraft. He was a fighter man. He "tolerated" only one four-engine bomber group.

After a few days, we were put on a B-24 and flown to Kunming, China, for assignment to a bomb squadron. On our way over the Hump to Kunming, I remember playing Red Dog, a form of poker game, on the flight deck of the B-24 at 18,500 feet. We had to share an oxygen mask among five of us because there weren't enough masks to go around. You got the mask when it was your turn to play.

At Chengdu, the crew was assigned to the 375th Bomb Squadron of the 308th Bomb Group, which was also part of the Chinese-American Composite Wing (CACW). The CACW existed as a combined first bomber, third fighter, and fifth fighter group with pilots from both the United States and the Republic of China. U.S. service personnel destined for the CACW entered the China theater in mid-July 1943. All U.S. pilots assigned to the CACW were listed as rated pilots in Chinese Air Force and were authorized to wear the pilot's wings of both nations.

I earned American Air Force pilot wings, of course, after I graduated from flight school. But I also qualified for, and wear, the Chinese Air Force wings. The Chinese do things a little bit differently from American flight schools. In America, when you graduate from flight school, they give you a set of orders, saying, "Okay, you're a pilot, you're in the Air Corps, and you can wear the wings," etc. The Chinese in Taiwan give you a document, but the wings they issue to you are serial numbered. If you write the Chinese Air Force and ask them who owns the wings with my serial number, they'll tell you William H. Drumm. They gave me two sets of orders to go with the wings, one in Chinese and the other in English. The Chinese wings, of course, are written in Chinese.

★ ★ ★ ★ ★

Achievements of the 308TH Bomb Group[109]

The 308th Bombardment Group (Heavy) had been activated on April 15, 1942. The 308th was moved to China early in 1943 as part of Gen. Claire Chennault's 14th Air Force. The missions of the 308th included supporting the Chinese by attacking airfields, coal yards, docks, oil refineries, and fuel dumps in French Indochina. It also mined rivers and ports and bombed shops and docks at Rangoon. The Japanese controlled most of the major ports in Southwest and Southeast China. Accordingly, the 308th attacked Japanese shipping in the East China Sea, Formosa Strait, South China Sea, and Gulf of Tonkin.

The 308th was composed of four bomb squadrons:

373 Bomber Squadron – Philippine Islands

374 Bomber Squadron – Rupsi

375 Bomber Squadron – Rupsi (Bill was assigned to this squadron.)

425 Bomber Squadron – Tezpur

The 308th Bombardment Group (Heavy) received a Distinguished Unit Citation (DUC) for an unescorted bombing attack against docks and warehouses at Hankow on August 21, 1943. The attack was conducted through heavy antiaircraft fire and fighter defenses. The unit received a second DUC for interdiction of Japanese shipping during 1944–1945. On one of the raids, on October 26, 1944, Maj. Horace S. Carswell Jr. was awarded the Medal of Honor for action. His story is well-worth reading. You can find it by using the endnote for this segment.

★ ★ ★ ★ ★

CHAPTER 11

Rupsi and the Missions

USAAF PHOTO

RUPSI, A SMALL village on the Bamaputra River, was located about 8.1 NM from Dhubri Town in Assam, India. The airfield was constructed prior to 1943 by the British to supply arms, manpower, and ammunition to the Allied forces. The British had built a 6,500 feet asphalt runway and some living structures. The Americans added a mess hall, a dispensary, a base exchange, clubs, administrative buildings, and living quarters. The base was located where the Assam River came down and turned and went south toward Calcutta.

Our quarters were straw huts called bashas. A basha was an open-air structure with a concrete floor and a straw roof. Each basha was large enough to sleep four people. The beds were wood with rope stingers supporting a thin mattress. Each bed had a mosquito net hung down on four sides. We all slept with a .45-caliber handgun under our pillows.

To ward off malaria, we had to take atabrine tablets every day. It was a major "campaign" on the base. They used "clever" poster to help you remember to take the pill.

Like Pandaveswar, it was controlled by the United States Army Air Forces Tenth Air Force and was the major transshipment facility in Assam Valley—the western terminus of transport routes "Able" and "Easy" into and returning from China. So back to India we went, to the old British base at Rupsi.

One night we were sleeping, and all of a sudden, about three o'clock in the morning, bang, bang, bang from someone's .45! Everybody ducked for cover. The next morning in the mess hall, I said, "What the world was going on last night? Who shot what?" and this one guy says, "About three o'clock I woke up, and here's these claws tearing at my mosquito net. This tiger was trying to get in bed with me! So I started shooting at him, and he ran away."

If he were like me, he couldn't hit the broad side of a barn with a .45 and would probably have better luck throwing the gun at the tiger!

★ ★ ★ ★ ★

Most meals were Spam and "C" rations. Once in a while, the cook would find a bunch of chickens on the open market, and that was always a welcome meal!

If we were flying, we would be issued a couple of boxes of "K" rations. One box either a breakfast, lunch, or dinner fare stuffed into a Cracker Jack box, along with a package of two cigarettes—Lucky Strikes, Camels, Old Golds, etc.

So our mission was hauling gas from Rupsi into China, mostly into Chengdu. A lot of people thought that B-29s were first used in Tinian and Saipan and the South Pacific. I don't believe so. I think B-29s were first in India. They were flying missions out of India, and they could get as far as the southern tip of Kyushu in Japan, which is where they were bombing, and it was to keep the Japanese awake, I think. After bombing, the B-29s couldn't get all the way back to India. They could get as far back as Chengdu, China, but they had to land and refuel there.

Everything that went into China during the war had to go by air over the "Hump" (the Himalaya Mountains in Burma), even toothpicks. Why? Because if you look at the map in 1932, the Japanese had taken over Manchuria. When they entered WWII, they sent troops down the coast to capture all the ports there. They also went into Indochina (Vietnam) and then around the horn and into Burma. That was where General Chennault initially had sent the P-40s and the people he had recruited from the States. He had sent them to an airfield just north of Rangoon to put the aircraft together and train the pilots.

We couldn't use any ports in China because of the Japanese occupation. So we had to take everything over the "Hump" using C-46s, C-109s, C-87s, and B-24s.

C-46 Commando USAAF photo

C-109 Liberator Express cargo version of B-24 (USAAF photo)

The C-109 had been designed to carry fuel. It had bladders in it for that contingency.

C-87 Liberator Express cargo version of B-24 (USAAF photo)

The C-87 was a B-24 converted to a cargo aircraft. They sent us in our B-24s to increase their capacity to send fuel into China for the B-29s. They were still using B-29s for bombing raids from Chengdu, even though they were flying also from Tinian and Saipan. In fact, they had even moved some of the B-29s into Chengdu and started letting them fly out of there, and we furnished the gas for those missions.

Flying the "Hump" over the Himalayan Mountains was pretty much routine, although occasionally, there were exceptions. The normal gross weight for the B-24 was around 58,000–60,000 pounds, depending on how it was configured and loaded. Most of our flights going over to China would take off with three 750-gallon bomb bay tanks loaded with aviation fuel at around 6:00 or 7:00 a.m. We would climb to 18,500 feet for a four-and-a-half-hour trip to China. (Field elevation at Rupsi was 131 feet above sea level.)

On most trips, we would land at either Kunming or Chengdu, unload the fuel, and return to Rupsi at 21,500 feet or higher, depending on the clearance and the weather.

Kunming Control Tower (USAAF photo)

Chinese laborers rolling the dirt for a runway
at Chengdu (USAAF photo)

By that time, in 1945, the Japanese had been cleared out of Northern Burma and were no factor. The enemy was weather. There were no radio ranges, light lines, VORs, ILS, or GPS facilities. There was one homer about 30 miles west of Kunming. On one occasion, I remember coming back around 1600 or so and running into a large thunderstorm just west of Kunming. At first, we were going up 2,400 feet per minute with the nose down and full power. Then without warning, we were going down at about the same rate with the nose high and full power!

Kunming Air Field (USAAF photo)

We had just landed at Kunming Air Base in China with our load of 115/145 gasoline. We decided to grab a quick bite while the gas was being off-loaded. It was already afternoon, so we were looking at a five or six o'clock takeoff for our return trip to Rupsi, India. As a "noncombat" flight, our crew was scaled down from eleven to five: pilot, copilot, navigator, flight engineer, and radio operator. We didn't need four gunners or a bombardier.

After finishing our snack, we stopped by weather to get a brief for our return flight. Of course, there would be thunderstorms and freezing levels to worry about. The weather people always had some joke about the weather that they thought was funny. This day was a little different. After the joke that wasn't funny, they got serious with us and asked us about our return flight plan, things like flight duration and how much return fuel we had.

When our aircraft was refueled, we were given only enough fuel to go straight from Kunming to Rupsi with a modest thirty-minute reserve. That translates into about five and a half hours of flying time. The point was, we didn't have extra fuel that would allow us to go around thunderstorms. We would have to go through them. The joke had been that the bad news was there were long lines of heavy thunderstorms all along our flight path, and we would be making our return trip in the dark of night. The "good" news was that because it would be dark, it would be easier to see what we would be trying to fly through! Not much consolation in that!

We walked out to our aircraft, completed our visual preflight, and boarded. No one mentioned the weather forecast. We ran the checklists, started the engines, and completed our various positional checklists as we taxied out to the runway. We received our clearance for immediate takeoff. As we advanced the throttles, I told the flight engineer, George Ronnenkamp, to keep an eye on the fuel.

Field elevation at Kunming was 6,207 feet. Our takeoff weight, around 40,000 pounds, was about 25,000 pounds below maximum gross for takeoff. As a result, the ground roll was not real long, and the liftoff was a piece of cake. As we settled into the climb profile, about 780 feet per minute, everyone relaxed a little as we passed over the big lake west of the field.

We reached our cruising altitude of 23,000 feet, leveled the aircraft, increased speed to cruise, and reset the throttles. We were on our way. The airplane was performing well, and the normal intercom conversations began.

About an hour and a half into the flight, as we scanned the skies in front of us, we saw it. The enemy! There, directly in front of us, was one of the biggest lines of thunderstorms I've ever seen. It was huge! We decided, as if we had a choice, to penetrate it and keep on going so we would have enough gas to get home.

As we drew closer and closer, the ominous sky grew darker and darker. It's bad enough to fly the Himalayas at night under the best of conditions, but flying through a violent thunderstorm over these mountains, with many mountains and 18,000 to 20,000 feet off your flight path, is beyond imagination. You would have to be there to believe it. The closer we got to the storm cloud, the smaller we felt! After all, I had flown these types of routes before. They just weren't as big as this one, and I hadn't seen this one's "teeth" yet.

But I had been warned. I took notes and could probably quote the whole briefing.

When we first arrived in theater, we were briefed that we would see, and fly through, some of the worst weather on the planet. And that was on a good day! The downdrafts were violent, the updrafts were violent, and high winds ranged between 120 and 200 knots. We planned to cruise at around 250 knots. If we encountered a direct headwind of 200 knots, then the aircraft would be moving forward in the air mass at 250 knots, but the air mass would be carrying the aircraft in the opposite direction at 200 knots. The net difference across the ground would be only 50 knots per hour. Our 1,200-mile trip, instead of taking about five hours, would take twenty-four hours!

Normal return routing (Charlie) from Kunming to Rupsi

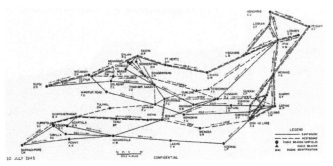

Photo by Jerry L. Burton

If there was any moisture in the air at all, icing was guaranteed above 20,000 feet, even on "nice" days. Icing on the lift surfaces, aka wings, not only adds weight to the airplane but also flattens the curvature of the wings, which is the "science" that produces lift.

One thing in our favor would be our weight. Our weight, after off-loading 13,500 pounds fuel at Kunming, was somewhere around 40,000 pounds. Maximum weight for takeoff was 65,000 pounds.

Suddenly, I was back to the "present." It felt like we had flown into a wall or hit another airplane or a ridge. Bam! Bam! The airplane was pitching and bucking like a wild animal. I fought just to hold the airplane straight and level. In my mind, I heard one of my instructors saying, "Fly the airplane! Fly the airplane!"

After a few minutes, things settled down. I quickly scanned my instruments, asked for a position report, and instructed the crew to strap on their parachute. I turned on all the outside lights so we could be seen by other aircraft that might be in the area. The flight engineer, George Ronnenkamp, quickly checked everyone's chutes.

Again, I scanned my instruments. Apparently, we had again flown through a wind shear and into a strong updraft. My rate of climb was 2,400 feet per minute, and the pitch attitude was nose level.

I pushed the nose downward to offset the effect of the updraft, reduced power, and lowered my flaps. My actions meant nothing to the updraft. We were still climbing at 2,400 feet per minute. I instructed the crew to hang on and make sure their belts and harnesses were as tight as they could get them!

It was dark outside, except for occasional lightning. There was no sense of motion, and we had no outside visual references! The force of the updraft pressed us hard into our seats.

Suddenly, I felt weightless, and the seat belt was pressing hard against my lap! I pulled the nose up and went to full power. We were still descending at an incredible rate! This was like riding a rodeo bull blindfolded!

Suddenly, we were going up again, and I had to push the nose over and reduce power. More wind shear! The airplane tried to roll to the left as we flew through another vertical wind shear! We were bouncing around like a rubber ball in a washing machine. A thousand particles began hitting the aircraft, creating a deafening noise that wouldn't go away. Hail!

I tried to focus on the instrument panel. Then I realized I was holding my breath! I consciously made myself breathe again. I reached over to the console and put my hand on the bail out toggle switch. In my mind, I quickly considered the consequences of a night bail out in a heavy thunderstorm over the highest mountains on earth. The updrafts were strong enough to keep our bodies airborne for a long time. The hail would break bone. The lack of oxygen would lead to death. Even if we made it to the ground, we would still have to deal with local tribes of head hunters in the villages below. But if we rode the aircraft into the ground or the aircraft broke up in flight, we all would surely die.

I looked over at my hand on the bail out switch. I thought to myself, *That bell better work!*[110]

After what seemed like an eternity, the lightning became intermittent, and the hail stopped.

We were actually straight and level for the first time since we took off. But it didn't last.

Suddenly we were back in the wind shear. Wow. Not bad. This was not nearly as violent as what we had first flown through. Maybe we were on our way out. I quickly scanned my instruments and descended back down to our assigned altitude.

The turbulence was intermittent, light to moderate. We suddenly got a break in the clouds. Then all of a sudden, we were back in them. Now we were clear again. Actually, we were flying in and out of the tops of cumulus clouds with a solid deck below us.

As we neared Myitkyina, we saw another line of thunderstorms. Our fuel was a little low, but I thought we were still okay. However, we were going to have to penetrate at least one more storm.

Pretty soon, the nightmare started all over again! Terrible turbulence and wind shear, thunder and lightning, up and down, pitching and yawing but not quite as bad as the first one. But there was one new twist.

The radio operator called me and said, "I've got a two-inch spark coming through the cable into my command set." I said, "How about your trailing antenna? Did you pull it in?" He replied, "Yes. I've had it in for about ten minutes, and I'm still getting sparks."

St. Elmo's Fire was running up and down the wings and jumping around on the propellers. We were still at 23,000 feet and getting quite a light shower outside on the aircraft. That would have been okay, but the sparks inside the aircraft could be what killed us. We

JERRY L. BURTON

had three bomb bay tanks for hauling fuel over to Kunming. The turbulence had been shaking the residual fuel in those tanks, and we were beginning to smell the fumes throughout the aircraft. Gas fumes and the sparks were not a good combination!

The radio operator suggested we descend to a lower altitude. Our minimum altitude in that area was 16,000 feet because we had 14,000-foot mountains below us.

So I dropped the gear, lowered some flaps, and turned on all our lights, inside and out. Then I pulled back the throttles to about 17 inches and put out a Mayday call, giving our position to all other aircraft in the area so they would know that we were leaving our assigned altitude.

As we leveled out at 16,000 feet, the static electricity went away, and our radios were working once again.

There was a C-46 in the area who called us on the radio. He had heard my Mayday and reported it to Myitkyina Control (ground tracking station). Myitkyina Control told him to relay instructions to us. Myitkyina had cleared us down to 16,000 feet just to make us "legal." We were to expect further clearance down to 10,000 feet over Myitkyina and then to 4,500 feet to Jorhat Control in the valley. Once we were in the Assam river valley, we could continue down the valley past Tezpur and to Rupsi at 4,500 feet.

It felt pretty good knowing that someone on the ground knew where we were and that we had been cleared all the way home.

When we got to Tezpur, we had scud clouds at our altitude. We flew on past Tezpur, and about ten minutes later, the engineer, George Ronnenkamp, told me, "We're not going to make it." I said, "We're not going to make it where?" He said, "Back home." I asked, "What's the problem?" He said bluntly, "We're going to run out of gas." I rolled immediately into a 180-degree turn and went back to Tezpur.

When we got back there, it was about ten or ten thirty at night. There was a C-46 base in the same area, Misamari. It was an Air Transport Command (ATC) base. I had the copilot circling around to the left so I could try to pick out our base between the clouds. I had to go into Tezpur, which was a Tenth Air Force Bomber Base.

As I was searching for the base, the copilot suddenly said, "Take over! Take over!" I looked at instruments and saw that we were in a thirty-degree bank, going down about 700 feet per minute, and number 3 engine was out. So I pulled back on the stick, straightened the airplane out, and hit the prop plate behind the propeller toggle switches and got all the engines up to 2,700 rpm. The number 3 engine, which was out of fuel, also went to 2,700 rpm. The engine had no gas in it, so when the gas hit that engine, it went up to 3,000 rpm. All of a sudden, I had more power on the right side than I did on the left side. It was just a matter of adjusting the rpm on all the engines. I quickly then made a decision on which field I thought was Tezpur. I entered a landing pattern as I was gradually losing airspeed down to pattern speed. I got on a final approach and made the landing. After we were on the ground, George Ronnenkamp told me, "You only had one engine on that landing and your final approach." It was kind of a surprise to me, but I wasn't interested. I was just interested in flying the airplane and getting it on the ground safely, which we did.

But trying to taxi it was another challenge. Number 1 engine was way out on the outside. I only had fuel enough to taxi on that one engine. I had to keep jockeying back and forth between the power and the rudder, trying to keep the thing moving straight.

We finally got it around to a parking space just in front of the tower, and there was a big telephone pole out there with a sign that read, "WATCH YOUR WING TIP." Well, guess what. I was watching the guy who came out to park us. All of a sudden, he started waving his hands to stop, and there was a jar of the airplane, and naturally, we had hit the telephone pole with our wing tip. It put a pretty good size gash in the outer wing panel.

So we shut down that one engine. The ground crew pulled the aircraft back with a tug and got it safely parked. The engineer George was up in the right-hand seat where the copilot switches were, and

JERRY L. BURTON

I asked George if the copilot had turned off all the switches. He put his head outside the window and said, "What did you say, sir?" Just about that time, the window fell out, hit the ground, and broke into smithereens!

At that point, I told the crew, "As far as I'm concerned, I've had enough for the night, and I don't know about you, guys, but I'm ready to go to bed." So we went to bed that night, and the next morning after breakfast, I went over to the aircraft engineering office. They had some B-24s on that base. I told the engineering officer that I needed a stellar wing panel and a copilot window.

And he said, "Oh, you do, huh?" And I replied, "Yes, sir." He then said, "Well, I'll tell you what. You just stick around here for another week or so, and we'll have one of these birds crash off the end of the runway, and we'll get you some parts."

So I went back to the crew and told them the story. We all agreed that that was not the answer to our problem. So I asked them, "Well, what do you think about flying the bird back with a hole in the wing and the window out? It's going to be a little drafty on the copilot's side, but other than that, I think the wing will hold up. That's just a guess on George's part and my part."

They all agreed, "Let's do it!" So we all got back in the airplane and took off and flew back down to Rupsi. It was forty-five minutes to an hour's ride down. I landed the airplane, and I wrote up, "Outer wing panel needs replacing and new copilot window," and walked away from the airplane. I went and had something to eat, and nobody ever said anything about it. They just replaced it all.

That was in World War II. You don't find people doing things like that today. They court-martial you or have an investigation, trying to figure out what happened, and make you pay for it.

★ ★ ★ ★ ★

The Making of a Hangar Queen

Speaking of missing parts, we had another interesting incident at Chengdu, China. We dropped off our load of fuel at Chengdu, and while going through the checklist before takeoff for our return to Rupsi, we noticed that the governor for the number 4 propeller was not functioning. I pulled back to the revetment across the runway, opposite base operations, where George determined, after a thorough examination, that we needed another governor. Naturally, there was not another governor on the field. I found another 308th bomb crew, explained our plight, and asked them to have our squadron maintenance send us another governor.

We all went to bed that night expecting to arise in the morning, have breakfast, and depart for home. Instead, when we went out to the aircraft, we found a generator and a few other items missing. It appeared that our aircraft was in danger of becoming a "hangar queen."

We had to have that generator and those other items to return to Rupsi. So again, I sent a request back to India. In the meantime, I got permission from operations to taxi the aircraft across the runway and park it closer to operations. We set up a two-hour watch for that night for each crew member. It was warm in Chengdu, so it was not a problem to spend a couple of hours at night out with the aircraft.

About 0300, George was lying down on the wing of the aircraft during his watch. Suddenly, he heard a "chug, chug, chug" sound approaching the aircraft. It was a vehicle known as a cherry picker. It was used to remove engines from aircraft.

It pulled up to one of the engines on our aircraft. George stood, pulled his .45 from the holster, and in no uncertain terms, stated, "The next person to move toward an engine on the aircraft will have his head blown off!" I don't know if those were his exact words, but needless to say, the cherry picker backed up and went "chug, chug, chugging" back in the direction from which it had come!

Three days later, we received our parts and were on our way back to India.

★ ★ ★ ★ ★

A Little R & R

I think it was probably in June or July that 1st Lt. William Cleveland "Cleve" Davis, another pilot in the squadron from Charlotte, North Carolina, and I were selected to go to Calcutta for a little R & R (rest and relaxation or rest and recreation). This flight was what was really called a whiskey run. The club officer asked us to pick up one case of gin, one case of White Horse scotch, and one case of bourbon for the club. He gave us 5,000 rupees (that was about $166) and instructions where to go in Calcutta and to contact Pete, a one-legged man in a store with a white front that looked like the front of a house.

So we flew down to the Calcutta airport—the actual name was Dum Dum. It was a military airport at the time, so that was where we stayed while we were down there. After we got settled at the airport, we headed into town. Following the instructions the club officer had given us, we got to the general area but couldn't find the store.

Finally, we saw a little kid sitting on a curb. We hoped he knew enough English to understand us and help us. So we asked him, "You know, little house . . . you know, white . . . store, you know . . . white?" Then in perfect English, he replied, "Oh yeah. It's across the street there." Boy did we feel dumb!

So we went across the street and into this little white store. There was a woman behind the counter when we walked in and asked for Pete. At first, she denied knowing any one by that name. After a little discussion, she wanted to know what we wanted with Pete, and when we told her we just wanted to buy a few cases of liquor, she told us to go next door and that he would be sitting on a stool.

Sure enough, when we walked in the store next door, there was Pete, with only one leg, sitting on a stool. As I recall, Pete was half Indian and half Italian. We told him we wanted a case of White Horse scotch, a case of gin, and a case of whiskey. Of course, this transaction was all legal because even though I was only twenty, Cleve Davis was twenty-two.

Pete asked if we had transportation because we would need to pick up the liquor at several different locations. We thought he had the liquor there at the store. But not that simple, so we went back out to Dum Dum. The motor pool sergeant at the base was very cooperative and let us borrow a weapons carrier, especially after we explained to him we would only have the vehicle about three hours. We figured those three hours were worth a bottle of White Horse scotch to the sergeant. He thought so too.

So back we went to the store with the white front. We picked up Pete, he threw three empty cases in the back end of the weapons carrier, and he gave us directions as to where to go. Maybe I should also mention that certain areas and streets in Calcutta were off-limits to GIs, and if you were caught in one, you were subject to a court-martial.

But we didn't let that bother us. We were on a mission. As we drove in and out of the restricted areas, Pete would have us stop; go in a home or store; retrieve two, three, or four bottles of liquor; and put them in the proper case, and then off we would go to another supply point. When the cases were full, we paid Pete the 5,000 rupees, dropped him back at the white store front, drove back to the base, loaded the liquor into the airplane, and locked it up. When we turned in the weapons carrier, we paid off the sergeant with a bottle of White Horse scotch and went back to town for dinner.

Not having had a good meal for about three or four months, Cleve and I were in the mood for a good steak dinner. We went to the "Great Eastern Hotel," which I believe was British owned and operated. We had a table on a balcony overlooking the main dining room and dance floor where the Brits were having a dinner dance. So we sat up there where we could see and hear the festivities below.

The British military had their families in India with them. India, at that time, had been a British colony for years. The dance was formal with the ladies in beautiful gowns and the men in formal dress uniforms. The next day, of course, the men would be back on the lines fighting.

Cleve and I started off our dinner with a half glass of Cognac, followed by a bowl of soup, fish, three filets of mignon each with accompanying vegetables, and a salad. The desert was a pie. Cleve took half, and I took the other half.

It was a very delightful dinner, and I believe the cost, with tip included, was $1.50 each. You can tell we really splurged. (Labor was very cheap at that time. We paid our houseboys five annas a month. The Brits in the area around Rupsi accused us of causing inflation; they only paid them three annas. I think one anna was equivalent to about two cents in U.S. currency.)

After dinner, we took a walk down the main street. We spotted a nightclub advertised as American. When we went in, the hatcheck girl explained that this was a private club, and we had to be members to get in. We were about to leave when an American gentleman walked up and introduced himself as the owner.

During our conversation, he asked us what kind of flying we were doing, where we came from, etc. He told us he was originally from Los Angeles. However, due to some unfortunate circumstances with the law enforcement authorities in the States, he was forced to leave. So he came to Calcutta and opened this club.

He invited us in to see the show and had the head waiter get us a table. All drinks and food we wanted would be on the house. We couldn't take him up on the food offer, but we did on the drinks. Needless to say, we took off for Rupsi late the next morning, but we had accomplished the "mission"!

★ ★ ★ ★ ★

Fog of War from the Time I Left the States to the Japanese Surrender

After the time Bill had completed crew training at Gowen, here's what happened in the Pacific and China Burma India Theater.

In the Islands

The U.S. Marines had made significant progress toward the recapture of islands for B-29 bases through battles at Iwo Jima on February 19 and Okinawa on April 1.

The Japanese had launched aircraft against the navy from Iwo Jima. The initial objective was to capture the airfield. It had been thought that Iwo Jima could possibly serve as a launching point for an invasion of Japan. The muddy volcanic beach sand made it unsuitable for a launch point. The airfield was improved by the Seabees, but used only as an emergency field was damaged U.S. aircraft.

Okinawa was important because of its proximity to Kyushu, only 350 miles. Capturing Okinawa was important in case the United States had to invade Japan.

The Japanese were determined not to surrender under any circumstances.

★ ★ ★ ★ ★

Over Japan

Over Japan, the pace of the bombing was stepped up. Then suddenly, the bombing was replaced on August 1 by a "leaflet" run. Several million leaflets were dropped over Hiroshima, Nagasaki, and thirty-three other Japanese cities to warn civilians of the destructive power of upcoming attacks. The atomic bomb was not mentioned, but the degree of destruction was stressed, and people were encouraged to flee their cities immediately. The message was in Japanese, and there was a list of twelve cities. The message also stated that possibly, cities not named on the leaflet could also be hit.

On August 6, 1945, the atomic bomb "Little Boy" was dropped on Hiroshima with devastating results.

New leaflets were prepared detailing the destruction of Hiroshima and noting that it was caused by only one bomb. By August 9, over five million of these leaflets were dropped over Japan. Later, on the ninth of August, the second atomic bomb, the plutonium bomb "Fat Man," was dropped on Nagasaki.[111]

The Japanese military and civilian governments were deadlocked on the issue of surrender. So no response was sent concerning the Potsdam offer.

Since no response had been sent to the United States, Nagasaki was bombed. Japan still was unable to get a consensus on surrender. The military branch said no, and the civilian branch said yes. At 2:00 a.m. on the tenth of August, the emperor, Hirohito, played his deity card and dictated a surrender.

By 7:00 a.m. on the tenth, the Japanese foreign minister had dispatched a message announcing their decision to the United States, China, Great Britain, and the USSR.

However, the Japanese people knew nothing of the surrender. So President Truman ordered the bombing of military targets to resume. New leaflets were printed and dropped on August 11 so the Japanese people would be aware that the emperor had surrendered and the war would be over soon. The emperor's people worked out the details of the emperor staying in power. Finally, on the fifteenth of August, the emperor publicly announced his capitulation.[112]

The war with Japan was over.

★ ★ ★ ★ ★

CHAPTER 12

The End and The Wind Down

A S A RESULT of the dropping of the atomic bombs on Hiroshima and Nagasaki on August 6 and August 9, respectively, the Japanese surrendered on August 15, 1945. We, of course, did not know at the time about the atomic bombs, only that the Japanese had surrendered. The formal agreement was signed on board the battleship Missouri in Tokyo Bay on September 2, 1945. Combat units stood down and began to return to the States.

Prior to the signing of the formal surrender, the Japanese had asked the Soviet Union to try to negotiate better surrender terms for them. What the Japanese didn't know was that the Soviet Union was buying time until August 8, the day before the United States dropped the second atomic bomb on Nagasaki. The Soviet Union invaded Manchuria the next day as the United States was dropping the bomb. Japan saw the futility of their situation and surrendered.[113]

Despite the cessation of hostilities with Japan, we continued to haul gas into China. We would fill all our 750-gallon tanks with fuel, fly it to various bases in China, and then fly back to India and repeat the same process. I think what we were doing was supporting Chang Kai-shek because he knew the Chinese Communists would start coming down from the north, and he was trying to develop his own air force and his own army to counteract them. That wasn't too successful, of course. He finally ended up in Taiwan, which at that time was called Formosa.

The group was ordered back to the United States in mid-October, but it was November by the time we finally left India. By that time, our crew had accumulated a total of twenty-seven missions. A trip over the Hump and back was considered one mission.

FOG OF WAR – 1945 –
WHAT HAPPENED WHILE I WAS IN INDIA

Liberation of concentration camps, such as Auschwitz, made the extent of the Holocaust clearer to the Allies. Bombs still fell on London and Germany in 1945, but before April was over, two of the Axis leaders, Mussolini and Hitler, would be dead. Mussolini was shot and then hung up for display in the town Dresdsquare. Hitler committed suicide.

Franklin D. Roosevelt died on April 12 but of natural causes.

The last major battle in Europe was the Battle of Berlin. It began on April 16, 1945, and lasted until May 2, 1945. German forces started surrendering as early as April 29. On May 7, 1945, the Act of Military Surrender was signed by Gen. Alfred Jodl, chief of staff, German Armed Forces High Command. The official end of hostilities was set for 2301 Central European Time, May 8, 1945.

The war in Europe was over! Germany's formal surrender followed on May 7, 1945.

President Truman, United States; Clement Atlee, Great Britain; and Joseph Stalin, Soviet Union, met from July 17 through August 2, 1945, at Potsdam to discuss the details of the conditions of surrender to be presented to Germany and Japan when they actually surrendered.

President Truman, a staunch anti-Communist, and Joseph Stalin, a Communist dictator, disagreed on many of the conditions. Stalin wanted to increase his Communist influence beyond his own borders, and Truman wanted to prevent that. So there you have the backdrop for the upcoming "Cold War."

★ ★ ★ ★ ★

THE WAR IN THE PACIFIC IN 1945

The war in the Pacific continued, but now the Allies could apply maximum force.

Prior to the surrender of Germany, the Japanese had received very little pushback from the United States. The Pacific theater was more reasonably a naval and air environment than a land army environment. As a result, the combatants were primarily navy, marine, and Army Air Force.

Some of the naval assets in Atlantic could be redistributed to the Pacific. This was also true of Army Air Force assets. If and when an invasion of Japan became necessary, then all army forces would have to be employed.

Another important factor, though, was the atomic bomb. On July 16, 1945, at Trinity Site near Alamogordo, New Mexico, the United States successfully tested the first atomic bomb. [114]

By the end of February 1945, the United States had attacked the Japanese in Manila, recaptured Bataan in the Philippines, and invaded Iwo Jima.

By March 10, U.S. airborne troops recaptured Corregidor in the Philippines, captured Manila, firebombed Tokyo using 279 B-29s, and invaded Zamboanga Peninsula on Mindanao in the Philippines.

Ten days later, the British liberate Mandalay, Burma. A week later, B-29s lay mines in Japan's Shimonoseki Strait to interrupt shipping.

In the first seven days of April 1945, the final amphibious landing of the war occurred as the U.S. Tenth Army invaded Okinawa, B-29s flew their first fighter-escorted mission against Japan with P-51 Mustangs based on Iwo Jima, and U.S. carrier-based fighters sank the super battleship *Yamato* and several escort vessels that planned to attack U.S. forces at Okinawa.

On April 12, 1945, President Roosevelt died and was succeeded by Harry S. Truman.

On May 8, 1945, victory was declared in Europe. Anticipating an invasion of their homeland, the Japanese, on May 20, began the withdrawal of their troops from China. They were right to do that because on May 25, the U.S. Joint Chiefs of Staff approved Operation Olympic, the invasion of Japan, and scheduled it for November 1.

In response, the Japanese premier Suzuki announced on June 9 that Japan would fight to the very end rather than accept unconditional surrender.

By the end of June, Japanese resistance on Okinawa and in the Philippines had ended.

On July 10, one thousand bomber raids began against Japan. Four days later, the U.S. Navy began bombardment of Japanese home islands.

On July 16, 1945, the first atomic bomb was successfully tested in New Mexico. Then on July 26, the components of the atomic bomb "Little Boy" were unloaded at Tinian Island in the South Pacific.

The Japanese, still struggling to gain a position for comprise at peace talks, sink the cruiser *Indianapolis*. This resulted in the loss of 881 crewmen. The ship sank before a radio message could be sent out, leaving survivors adrift for two days. The ship had been struck by a Japanese submarine.

I learned in school that Pres. Theodore Roosevelt had coined the phrase, "Speak softly and carry a big tick." The United States had attempted to redirect Japan before the war. Japan chose to seek power through force and become an empire rather than to choose influence through economic alliances. We had spoken softly. Now on July 16, 1945, we had a big stick. The United States successfully detonated the first atomic bomb.

On July 26, 1945, President Truman issued the "Potsdam Declaration." In it, he warned Japan that if it "did not surrender, it would face 'prompt and utter destruction.'"[115]

There was no surrender. So on August 6, 1945, the first atomic bomb was dropped on Hiroshima from the B-29 named *Enola Gay* flown by Col. Paul Tibbets. Most people know that the *Enola Gay* was named after Colonel Tibbets's mother, Enola Gay Tibbets.[116]

On August 8, 1945, the nonaggression pact between the USSR and Japan ended. The USSR declared war on Japan and invaded Manchuria. The next day, August 9, the second atomic bomb was dropped, this time on Nagasaki, by another B-29, "Bock's Car," flown by Maj. Charles Sweeney. Emperor Hirohito and Japanese prime minister Suzuki decided to seek an immediate peace with the Allies.

On August 14, 1945, the Japanese accepted an unconditional surrender, and General MacArthur was appointed to head the occupation forces in Japan. Two days later, General Wainwright, who had been a POW since May 6, 1942, was released from a POW camp in Manchuria.

On August 27, 1945, airdrops of supplies to Allied POWs began. Supplies were dropped to POW in China and Korea. Unfortunately, the Soviet Union shot down a B-29 dropping supplies to POWs in Korea.

The occupation of Japan began on August 29 with the landing of the first U.S. troops near Tokyo. The next day, the British moved back to Hong Kong.

Official surrender ceremonies were conducted on September 2, 1945, aboard the Battleship *Missouri* in Tokyo Bay as one thousand carrier-based planes flew overhead. President Truman declared V-J Day.

It took about eleven days before the outlying Japanese units, including the Philippines, Wake Island, Singapore, Korea, and Burma, surrendered.

On October 24, 1945, the United Nations was born.

★ ★ ★ ★ ★

JERRY L. BURTON

GOING HOME

As I heard it, losses of the CBI teams in ATC, Tenth Air Force, amounted to over six hundred aircraft and over one thousand airmen. I don't know what the losses were the Fourteenth Air Force over the Hump.

The return plan for aircrews was based on time in theater. Those crews who had been in theater the longest were the first crews who got to go home. The plan also sought to let aircrew return to the States in the airplanes they had flown in theater. However, by this time, there were more aircrews than there were planes because not every aircrew, like mine, had flown an aircraft over from the States. In addition, there were ground crew and other nonflying personnel who needed to go home. So some people in the squadron got to fly, and others had to go by boat.

When an aircraft was being flown home, the entire crew would be included as well as a second pilot and copilot from another crew. From my crew, the copilot and I were chosen to fly back in "Hump Time," along with Bill Davis's crew and some other squadron ground personnel who had been in India for a long time. The bombardier and the rest of our crew went home by boat.

Bill Davis and his crew had originally flown "Hump Time" from the States to India. "Hump Time" was just one of several B-24s I had flown over the Hump.

Some of the B-24s I had flown were E-, J-, and M-models. Our ultimate destination was Morrison Field, West Palm Beach, Florida.

B-24J   B-24E

B-24M

Since Bill Davis was senior to me, having been in the squadron longer, he chose to fly the first leg back, which was from Rupsi to Karachi, India. Our final destination for our return was Morrison Field, West Palm Beach, Florida.

For some reason, I didn't know why, I began getting sick in flight. I kept getting sicker as we went. We got into the traffic pattern at Karachi, and I just threw up all over the bomb bay. We landed, and I got out and went to see the medics at the airport. The next day, I saw a doctor. I told the doctor that I was supposed to fly the next day from Karachi to Abadan, Iran. The doc left for a minute. When he came back, he handed me some pills. He said, "Now take these pills after you take off. You should do okay, but when you get to Abadan, let the other pilot land the airplane." So I said, "Okay, fine."

I was pretty sick that night, but the next morning, I felt okay. So we got in the airplane about nine o'clock and began the start procedure. We always started number 3 engine first because it had the hydraulics on it—gear and stuff—and then number 4, and then number 2. When we got to number 1, it wouldn't start. It had a broken starter. We were told that it couldn't be fixed till after 1500. That was too late to take off because it would put us in Abadan after dark, and we were restricted from flying at night. That's funny, in a way. We were flying over the hump at night, bad weather and all, but couldn't do it on the way home.

I was really feeling lousy, so I popped the pills, figuring they would wear off by the next morning. They didn't seem to help, so I went back to the dispensary. The doctor took one look at me, went into the next room, and came back carrying a mirror. He held the mirror up in front of me and said, "Look at your eyeballs, face, and hands!" They all had a yellowish color. He said, "You have a good case of jaundice, and you're going to the hospital in town." There was a small clinic on the airfield, but the hospital was in Karachi, about five miles away. In the ambulance, I wrote a note, saying where I was being taken, and asked the driver to put it on any bed in the tent I was assigned to back at the airfield.

When I got to the hospital, I turned in my .45 and received a receipt (a turn-in slip) for it.

Three days later, Davis and the crew came by. They said they had been looking all over Karachi for me; evidently, the ambulance driver wasn't too reliable. Davis asked me how long I would be in the hospital. Just then, the doctor came by, and we asked him. He said at least three weeks. Then Davis said, "They've been on me to get the airplane out of here. And, uh, we're going to have to leave you here." I replied, "Well, okay." So the crew bid me farewell and left Karachi the next day without me.

After about three weeks, I was released from the hospital. The doctor told me not to drink any beer or anything like that for about six months.

I went back to the base and talked with the operations officer. I told him my airplane was gone and asked if there was any chance of getting on another airplane coming through here and getting back to the States. He looked at my orders and saw that they stated that I would go on back on a B-24. The orders listed the crew, and I was on them. The airplane, of course, had already gone, and I wasn't on it. So he told me that these orders were no good. He then instructed me to go back to personnel, and they would get me new orders.

I went to personnel, and the sergeant told me, "Come back in about a week, and I should have new orders for you. These are no longer any good, and I'll have to work it through Calcutta to get your new orders. Chances are nine out of ten that you'll be going home by boat." I asked him when the next boat was scheduled to leave. He told me it would be in March—more than four months from now!

★ ★ ★ ★ ★

JERRY L. BURTON

CHAPTER 13

Alone, Unafraid, and AWOL

S O I WAS sitting at the bar in the club one night drinking a beer I wasn't supposed to have, and these contract carrier pilots came in and sat beside me. I think they were either United or Pan American pilots. We started talking, and they asked me what I was doing here. I told them my story, that my airplane was gone, and I was in the hospital. The captain said, "Hey, if you can do it, get your bags packed and meet me down at operations at twelve o'clock. We have an airplane going through here. We'll get you on board that. It's a contract carrier, and it's called the Embassy flight."

I got down there a little before twelve o'clock. I knew the aerodrome officer. He was a first lieutenant from the barracks we were staying in. He walked over to me and said, "Bill, what the hell are you doing down here with all those bags?" I said, "Well, I haven't heard anything from personnel, but I do have this one set of orders." He said, "Let me see them." So I gave him the set of orders that showed "by B-24" and had my name on it. He took them from me and walked over and sat at the desk. He put my orders in the typewriter, x'd out "by B-24" and typed in "by contract carrier," and signed his name as operations officer. Then he added my name to the passenger manifest. When the aircraft came in, he handed the manifest to the pilot, and away we went.

I boarded the aircraft and settled in. The aircraft was a C-54 with plush seats; it was really nice. We took off with only four or five passengers on the airplane. Our first landing was in Athens, Greece.

Karachi to Athens

They changed crews there. I was introduced to the new crew and was having breakfast with them. Then a major came by and said, "Lieutenant, I'd like to see your orders." So I handed him my orders. This major was known for sending guys back who were doing what I was trying to do. It felt like he looked at my orders for thirty minutes. It was probably more like thirty seconds or so. Then he just handed them back to me and said, "Okay. You go ahead. Go on." I sighed a big sigh of relief.

From Athens, we flew to Rome, Italy.

There was a captain there who was known for the same thing as the major in Athens. We were on the ground for a couple of hours. I was relieved when we got back in the airplane and taxied out for takeoff. We took off, and at about three hundred feet above the ground, one of the right engines went out. We came back around and landed. The engine needed to be changed.

After disembarking, the crew pointed out the captain to me. I spent the next three days dodging the captain. But finally, the engine was changed, and the aircraft was ready to go. The crew somehow got me on the manifest without me having to appear before the captain. Needless to say, I was very relieved when we boarded the aircraft and took off.

From Rome, after circling the Leaning Tower of Pisa, we flew to Lisbon, Portugal. From there, we went to the Azores.

We landed at night in a dense fog. The crew was making an instrument approach. I was sitting by a window looking out into the black of a stormy sky. All of a sudden, the aircraft pulled sharply up as a red light passed quickly by the window. It was another aircraft going the other direction!

We landed without further incident. The next morning, we departed the Azores for Gander, Newfoundland.

The trip to Gander was the longest leg of the trip, and it was all over water. By the time we got to Newfoundland, it was night again. We landed, and a new crew entered the airplane. I was introduced to the new crew and told that they would be taking the airplane to New York the next morning. I asked them where they were hanging out, got just my shaving kit, and went and got a bunk in the same area with them.

The next morning, I woke up about nine o'clock. I walked over to one of the other bunks. I shook the guy and asked him when they were going to take off for New York. He looked up at me and said, "Ohhhh. We forgot all about you! We changed crews again last night, and the airplane is already gone!" B-4 bag, parachute bag, all my clothes—gone!

So I quickly dressed and ran down to operations. There was a military C-54 just about ready to taxi for takeoff. I ran out and climbed the ladder and asked, "Can I go back to New York with you?" "Yeah," he said. "Get your name on the manifest. We're about ready to go." So I ran back to operations, got my name on the manifest, and then ran back out to the airplane. They were just about ready to pull up the ladder, but I got on. I walked into the cabin, expecting the plush seats. Boy, was I disappointed! This was a military plane, one that had those damn web seats along the side that were designed to hold a parachute that was slung under your rear end. It was terrible—just terrible!

We got to New York City at 12,500 on top. The weather was solid all the way down to 1,000 feet. The crew said it was going to be five or six hours before we could get down. The captain said, "We're not going to just sit up here. Washington National (now Reagan International) is open. We're going to divert to Washington, land and refuel, and then go VFR (visual flight rules) under the clouds back to New York." So we went to Washington National and landed.

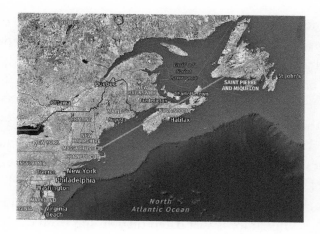

It just so happened that at that time, my cousin, Bernice Krause, was a Navy WAVE and was working in Fleet Admiral King's office. I called and told her that I was in Washington but had to go back to New York to get my bags and things. After that, I'd like to come back down, if that was okay with her, and stay a few days and see Washington, DC and visit. She agreed.

We were on the ground about two hours. Then we took off for New York. We were able to fly under the ceiling and landed at La Guardia at about ten o'clock that night.

We got off the airplane and walked inside. I saw one of the customs boys standing around in uniform. I went over to him and asked him, "Hey, did you happen to see a B-4 bag and a parachute bag come in here sometime today?" He said, "Yeah, there are a couple of bags over there by that post. They've been sitting here all day. Take a look at them." I went over there, and sure enough, they were mine. So I just picked them and walked out of the place, right in front of the customs guy. Those were the good ol' days!

I stayed at Fort Totten that night. Then I caught a train the next day down to Washington, DC. I wasn't going to take any chances on weather. I stayed there and visited with my cousin for about three days. We visited all the monuments and places of interest in the capital. We went to the building where my cousin worked and met Admiral King in the hallway.

On the third day, I thought I'd better check with the Army Air Forces and determine what my status was. So I went over to personnel at Bolling Field. I spoke with a major. He said, "Let me see your orders." I handed him my orders and the turn-in slip for my .45. He looked at them, and I told him where all I had been. He said, "Is this all you've got?" I said, "Yes." He looked down at my orders and then back up at me and said, "Well, I'm not sure, but I think that since you were supposed to return to the States with a crew on a B-24, which was supposed to land at Morrison Field in West Palm Beach, Florida, you've been AWOL for about a month now. Your only saving grace is that dated turn-in slip from the hospital in Karachi. If I were you, I'd get my butt down to West Palm Beach, Florida, in one big hurry."

I thanked him and appreciated the fact that he did not call the military police to escort me to be sure I took the next train south to the land of Florida! Needless to say, I kissed my cousin goodbye and took the next train going to West Palm Beach.

When I arrived at Morrison Field, I went directly to the base personnel office and reported in to a captain. I told him what I'd been doing and told him, "I give up."

He said, "I'll tell you what. Go get a room at the BOQ, here are the directions to the officers' club, enjoy our beaches, and report back here once a day for new orders. In about a week, we should have orders placing you on R & R" (rest and recuperation for forty-five days). I said, "Will I get court-martialed?" He responded, "No. Just make sure you come back to get your orders." I almost dropped my eye teeth but managed to thank the gentleman and was on my way to enjoy the beach.

So I checked every day for a week and no orders. Then I went to see the personnel officer again. "You don't have the orders yet?" I asked. "No," he answered. "We're having difficulty verifying your entry into the United States. We sent a telegraph to New York, and they said they never heard of you."

So I answered, "Well, I didn't land at New York. I landed at Washington first. Is that a problem?" "Oh, you landed at Washington first?" he asked. "Yes, I landed at Washington," I confirmed. "Well," he said, "come back this afternoon, and I'll have new orders for you." So when I went back, he had the orders.

Then the captain told me to go down to the train station and show them my orders. Because certain railroads had agreements with the federal government, for eleven bucks, I was able to get a ticket that took me to Fort Benjamin Harrison, now Camp Atterbury, in Indianapolis, Indiana. My parents were living in La Porte, Indiana, at the time, so I hitchhiked the last leg since there was no direct rail transport between Indianapolis and La Porte at that time.

When I was getting out of the service, I was actually reimbursed for 1,400 miles at five cents a mile for that trip to Fort Benjamin Harrison.

At that time, railroads were the most popular and affordable means of transportation. There was no production of automobiles for the general public during the war, and there were no car rental agencies. Commercial aviation was in its infancy and very expensive, especially for a first lieutenant making only about $291 a month.

By the time I got home, it was almost Christmas 1945. I spent the holiday with the folks. Merry Christmas!

★ ★ ★ ★ ★

CHAPTER 14

Mary Lou

MY ROOMMATE FROM St. Benedict's lived in Chicago. I called him, and we decided it would be a marvelous idea if we drove his parents' car to Kansas City and met with Mary Lou and the girl he had been dating before we went to war. New Year's Eve in KC we took the girls to dinner and dancing and had a wonderful reunion.

In January, I had to report to Greenville, North Carolina, to be discharged. So I traveled all the way back to the East Coast. We did all the paperwork discharging me from active duty. My release from active duty would be in March 1946. I did additional paperwork, which placed me in the AF Reserve. I would be doing my flying out of Fairfax, a suburb of Kansas City, Kansas. The reserves had AT-6s there. (After about seven hours of flying with them, I was made an instructor pilot).

Paperwork done, they told me, "Okay, you're a civilian now. Go home." And I did.

I got home and decided that I wanted to see Mary Lou again, so I took the train back to KC about a month later, got a job with Skelly Oil Company in Kansas City, and stayed. She was in her final semester at Mount St. Scholastica in Atchison, Kansas.

During the week, Mary Lou was in classes, and I worked during the day. On weekends, I would jump on a train and go up to Atchison and stay with one of the guys in the boys' dormitory. Mary Lou and I would date on the weekends, and then I'd go back down to Skelly. However, I really tried not to bother Mary Lou too much because she was on a scholarship and carrying a heavy study load.

In February, Mary Lou and I became engaged. She graduated cum laude on May 30 with a bachelor of science in mathematics and a minor in economics. I have her graduation certificate displayed on the wall. I like to invite people to read it and see what she majored in. Of course, the catch is that it is printed entirely in Latin.

We were married on June 6, 1946, at St. Margaret Mary Church in Chicago, where I had gone to grammar school. We honeymooned at Tabor Farm in Sodus, Michigan, where we met two friends who had gotten married the previous day.

I got a job in Kansas City, and that fall, I enrolled at St. Benedict's. I, like so many returning GIs, started a whole new life under the GI Bill on $90 a month.

We did supplement our income though. I worked at J. C. Penney's after school and on weekends, and Mary Lou kept books for the Suzie-Q restaurant. During the summer months when we were out of school, I worked for Pillsbury Mills, loading one-hundred-pound sacks of flour into boxcars.

David, our first son, came along in May 1947. I had finished my junior year and had additional credits from the University of Missouri-Kansas City and Michigan State, which I earned when I was in the military, courses like navigation and so forth. University of Missouri-Kansas City recognized the St. Benedict and Michigan State credits. This meant that I could graduate earlier if I consolidated all my credits at U of M-KC. So in January 1948, we moved to Kansas City, where I entered the University of Kansas. Our second son, Michael, joined us in May 1948. With our family increasing in numbers, I was trying to get out of school as fast as I could.

About a year earlier, Pres. Harry Truman had signed the National Security Act of 1947. This is the act that created a new branch of service, the United States Air Force.

I was still in the reserves, and in April of my senior year, I heard that the military was looking for more pilots. Naturally, I submitted my application to go back on active duty. Most of the guys I talked to assured me that I wouldn't get called up for at least a year or a year and a half. That was going to work great!

Unfortunately for me, that turned out NOT to be the case.

About September, I got my "report for duty" letter. They were telling me to go to Great Falls, Montana, in October for airlift training, and after that, I would be going to Germany.

I was really irritated about being called up so soon. I only needed twenty-two more credit hours to complete my bachelor's degree. Now that was going to be put on hold, and I had to leave for Great Falls. What on earth was so critical that they had to have me deploy so quickly?

★ ★ ★ ★ ★

JERRY L. BURTON

CHAPTER 15

The Berlin Crisis

POSTWAR GERMANY[117]

AFTER WORLD WAR II ended, the Soviet Union controlled all of Eastern Europe except Berlin. Stalin wanted badly to control all of Berlin to complete his empire.

Because the Soviet Union had been given responsibility for East Germany and Berlin was deep inside East Germany, the Soviet Union authorized limited access from West Germany into West Berlin by road, rail, and waterway. Additionally, there were three air routes used for access to West Berlin from West Germany. The primary method of moving supplies from West Germany through East Germany into West Berlin was by road and rail. Note the map above.

The Soviet Union wanted the United States, Britain, and France sectors of West Germany to pay war reparations to them in the form of cash, industrial equipment, and natural resources. They also wanted a "neutral" and disarmed defeated Germany.

The United State, Great Britain, and France, the Allies who controlled West Germany, thought otherwise. So in May 1946, the United States quit paying the war reparations to the Soviet Union. Soon after, Britain and France also quit paying. Of course, this upset the Soviet Union, and negotiations to resolve the conflict among the four countries began.

Work began to devise a relief plan that involved the institution of a new monetary system. The United States was the central "player" in the development of this system. Even the name of the currency and the design of the money was developed in the United States. The goal of this plan, in the mind of the United States, was to see Germany develop into a viable partner in the European economy.

The major problem with this plan, in the view of the Soviet Union, was the introduction of a new currency into West Berlin. The Soviet Union had hoped to eventually force or "persuade" the other three Allies to abandon West Berlin and unify the city under Soviet control. The Western-style economy of West Berlin would make that more difficult.

Negotiations continued until two years later, on June 22, 1948, the negotiations broke down.

THE BERLIN BLOCKADE[118]

On June 24, the Soviet Union blocked the roads, rail lines, and waterways into West Berlin.

In just two days, on June 26, 1948, the Berlin Airlift began. I believe the strategy of an airlift was put forth immediately, perhaps by President Truman himself or by Stuart Symington, secretary of the newly formed U.S. Air Force. The general feeling at that time was that our air force could move anything. In the China Burma India Theater, we were moving food, machinery, weapons, ammunition, and people, and my crew and I and others like us were hauling highly flammable aviation gas. We did this over the highest mountains in the world in the worst weather on the planet with the crudest of navigation aids. Each of my flights covered more than 750 miles one way and took four hours. We landed at Kunming, China, checked weather for the return flight while our cargo was being off-loaded, and then flew another four hours back to Rupsi, India, in the dark.

JERRY L. BURTON

According to historian Francis Pike in his book *Hirohito's War: The Pacific War, 1941–1945*,[119] at least 700 Allied planes got shot down or crashed, and over 1,200 airmen lost their lives. Expressed another way, one of every three aircrew lost his life.

In the Berlin Airlift, remarkable men did remarkable things too. Their trips were probably an average of 200–300 miles one way. Some crews made as many as three round trips in one day! The total tonnage for the thirteen- or fourteen-month operation was 395,000 tons. At the height of the operation, one aircraft was landing in Berlin every sixty seconds.[120]

MY ASSIGNMENT

My assignment to Great Falls, Montana, was as a four-engine pilot in preparation for further assignment to the Berlin Airlift. Two days before I was supposed to leave, I received a telegram from the Pentagon, diverting me to the 509th Bomb Wing at Walker AFB in Roswell, New Mexico. In a way, this was a blessing. Mary Lou and the kids could join me. That would not have been possible with the airlift assignment. In addition, Mary Lou, having lived in Kansas City and Atchison most of her life, had a bad sinus problem. The high, dry climate of Roswell cured the problem within a week of her arrival.

After reporting to the 509th, I learned that there had been twelve other lieutenants and captains diverted to the 509th. It was, of course, the 509th that had dropped the two atomic bomb on Japan and, later on, several Pacific test sites. At the time, it was the only combat-ready wing with nuclear experience.

When we arrived, we were told that the base was on an eighteen-hour alert. If the "whistle blew" when we were on a six-hour alert, the B-29s would be loaded up with all essential maintenance equipment and personnel and then flown to England. There, they would land, pick up ordnance, and proceed to targets. We were not briefed on where the targets would be.

The world situation was chaotic with everyone on edge. This could have been part of an exercise or real world. World War II had just ended, and Russia still had a formidable standing military and had acquired their own nuclear capability. Russia was Communist, and many saw Russia as the next adversary; Communism was a dirty word in those days.

I didn't know what the Russians were up to or why. There were "theories" and rumors, of course. But the only official knowledge I had concerned only those things that directly affected me. For example, I knew that the Russian military had blockaded all avenues for moving supplies by ground (road, rail, and canal) to the non-Russian occupation forces in Berlin. I knew that as a result of this action by the Russians, I could, on a moment's notice, find myself involved in a major, top-priority logistics action that could be either practice or real. What the Russians were trying to accomplish by this action was something of a mystery to all of us.

One of the "theories" that circulated involved the presidential election, which was less than a week away. The major contenders were Democratic candidate president Harry S. Truman and Republican candidate, governor of New York State, Thomas E. Dewey. Both candidates ran hard-fought, no-punches-barred public campaigns. The candidates were neck to neck with Dewey slightly favored to win. In some circles, it was thought that such a division of the country might be construed as a weakness of our nation's resolve.

In any case, the base actually did get down to a six-hour alert. The "whistle" never blew, we never went, and I didn't know any specifics of what information or actions were driving the changes in the alert status while I was there.

Fog of War: What I didn't know was that the Soviet Union immediately began building up their forces in and around Berlin.

In a matter of weeks, the Soviet army of occupation in East Germany had increased to forty divisions. The Allied sectors stood at eight divisions.

President Truman sent some B-29s to Britain. Tension remained high, but war did not break out. The Soviet Union on May 12,

1949, lifted the blockade of West Berlin. The United States, Great Britain, and France continued to supply the West Berlin by air for several months in case the Soviets decided to resume the blockade. The Berlin Blockade was the first major multinational skirmish of the cold war.[121]

★ ★ ★ ★ ★

LIFE BETWEEN WARS

So that was my return to active duty. After the Berlin crisis was resolved, they assigned me to maintenance as a maintenance officer. Later, they moved me to supply because the guy who was the supply officer, who was also a pilot, was going to Fort Worth to be trained as an engineer on a B-36.

I was a first lieutenant and totally unfamiliar with the supply duties. So I just signed for all the equipment that the paperwork said we should have. About three or four weeks later, I was informed that supply was missing a bunch of sheets, jackets, wrist watches, etc. I was, of course, pretty upset. So one of the sergeants came to me and said, "Lieutenant, we can make this up. It might cost a little bit, but we can do it." I asked him, "How are you going to do it?" He answered, "Well, we'll turn some of our old sheets in for exchange, you know, the worn-out ones, and we'll also include other shortages. And of course, we have to put a bottle of whiskey in with the bundle."

Well, we finally got all the shortages made up. When the previous supply officer came back, we were at the bar one night, and I told him what we had done. He said, "Oh, I knew there were shortages, but I didn't know it was that much! How much did it cost you?" I told him, "It cost me forty-eight bucks." He replied, "Okay. Here's twenty-four." So we split the difference!

Then in recognition of my shortcomings as a supply officer, they sent me to supply school at Lowry AFB up in Denver. We were the last class to use that particular classroom at Lowry. The next group to use it was the first class of USAF Academy cadets. The Air Force Academy in Colorado Springs was under construction but had not been finished yet.

★ ★ ★ ★ ★

Getting the Short Straw

It was around April 1949. I had been back on active duty for about a year and a half as a reserve officer. The world seemed to have stabilized, to some degree, so the government decided to initiate a RIF. RIF stands for "reduction in force."

Reserve officers were more vulnerable for release than were active duty officers. There was the perception that active duty officers were more valuable and authentic; they were "career" officers. That perception hardly exists today.

There were four first lieutenants in the group. The group commander called all of us into his office. I was from the maintenance squadron, another one was from engineering, and one was the group commander's adjutant. I don't remember where the other guy was assigned. The group commander, Colonel Randolph, said, "I can't tell the difference between any of you, guys. You're all the same as far as I'm concerned, but I've got to pick one of you to be RIFd. The only way I can do it is by drawing straws." I was really worried. I had two young boys and my pregnant wife at home to take care of.

So the adjutant got the straws all fixed up for us to draw. Just before we started to draw, I said, "Colonel, if I'm not mistaken, I think I'm on orders to go to Japan." The colonel replied, "You're what?" I answered, "I think I'm on orders to go to Japan." The colonel turned to his adjutant and told him, "Call wing personnel and check that out." The adjutant made the call and then informed the colonel, "Yeah, he's right, Colonel. He's going to Japan. He's on orders already. They just haven't been issued yet."

Then the colonel addressed me, "Okay. Sorry, Drumm. I'm wrong. You're going to have to get out of here. I can't include you." As I was leaving, the engineering guy popped up and said, "Hey, Colonel, I think I'm on orders too." I don't think they even bothered to check with personnel on him.

Later, I found out that when they drew straws, the colonel's adjutant drew the short straw!

★ ★ ★ ★ ★

CHAPTER 16

To Japan and the Korean War

AFTER JAPAN HAD surrendered, it was placed under international control. Gen. Douglas MacArthur had been made the supreme commander in charge of the reconstruction of Japan. Japan was not allowed to have any kind of military forces. Consequently, the United States had to ensure the security of the nation. To facilitate that, U.S. forces were stationed in Japan.

So I was sent over to Japan. My family was supposed to accompany me, but just two weeks prior to leaving, my family was removed from the orders. It should have told me something about the trouble brewing on the world scene.

Also, instead of going to Iwakuni Air Base, just southwest of Hiroshima, where I was to receive training as a pilot on C–54s, I was assigned to the 621st Aircraft Control and Warning Center Squadron at Niigata, just over halfway up Japan and on the west coast. I had been to supply school, and the air force had an opening for a supply officer in the 621st, so I was sent there instead.

I arrived in Japan in May 1950. On June 25, North Korean troops invaded South Korea. The same day, South Korean president Syngman Rhee purportedly executed one hundred thousand people, fearing that they were all Communists. Two days later, the United

Nations sent troops, which included Americans, into South Korea. The Korean War had begun!

Niigata was a radar station with three slave sites along the coast off the Sea of Japan and one site on an island just off the coastline. We were like the air control centers in the States except for the word "warning," which implied that we were alert for enemy aircraft approaching. Japan was in range of North Korean and Russian aircraft, and things were beginning to heat up in that region.

I had just had a nice breather from combat and threat of combat. Europe was tense, but it didn't seem to me that conflict was imminent. And now I had been sent to Japan with no idea why there was suddenly conflict there.

Fog of War: The Korean peninsula had been a Japanese colony from 1910 through the end of World War II. After surrendering to the Allied powers—Great Britain, the Soviet Union, France, and the United States—Japan lost control of Korea.

Interestingly, the Soviet Union had not joined the Alliance against Japan until peace was imminent. In fact, the Soviet Union and Japan had signed a five-year nonaggression pact in April 1941. This agreement enabled Japan, eight months later, to attack the United States at Pearl Harbor without the Russians getting involved.

No other nation in Asia posed a threat to Japanese expansion. The pact allowed the Soviet Union to concentrate on protecting itself from Germany without getting "backdoored" by Japan.

The German threat to the Soviet Union ceased on May 7, 1945, when Germany signed an unconditional surrender.

On August 6, 1945, the United States dropped the first atomic bomb on Hiroshima. Japan was indicating that it would not surrender. An Allied invasion could lead to the loss of many U.S. military personnel. Pres. Harry Truman asked Joseph Stalin to declare war on Japan, hoping that the threat of a double invasion of Japan would hasten a surrender. He was right. The Soviet Union, two days later, on August 8, 1945, at 11:00 p.m., renounced the nonaggression pact with Japan. Furthermore, the Soviet Union declared war on them, effective 0001, on August 9, 1945.

So at one minute past midnight, August 9, 1945, Russia launched three simultaneous invasions of Manchuria from the east, west, and north. For the Soviet Union, the objective of these invasions was to gain territory that had previously been contested between Japan and the Soviets.

At one minute past midnight Trans-Baikal time on August 9, 1945, the Soviets commenced their invasion of Manchuria simultaneously on three fronts from the east, west, and north of Manchuria. Between August 9 and September 2, a period of three weeks and three days, the Soviets were able to occupy Manchuria/ Manchukuo, Inner Mongolia/Mengjiang, Sakhlin, the Kuril Islands, and Northern Korea. Much of this territory had been lost to the Japanese in the Russo–Japanese War of 1904–1905.

At 11:02 a.m. on August 9, 1945, the second atomic bomb ever used in war was dropped on Nagasaki. Between the Russian attack on the continent and the atomic bomb in Japan itself, the war was over. Japan surrendered and agreed to sign an unconditional surrender on September 2, 1945. However, Japan had one request—the retention of Hirohito as emperor. Their request was granted.

Russia was a big winner. They recovered more than they had lost in China to Japan. In Korea, they were allowed to remain in the northern part of Korean down to the Thirty-Eighth parallel.

CONFLICT BETWEEN NORTH AND SOUTH[122]

The Soviet Union had been given the responsibility for disarming and establishing a system of government in North Korea. The North Korean Communist leader was Kim Il-Sung. The Russians began to withdraw.

The United States had the responsibility to do the same in South Korea. The South Korean government was led by Dr. Syngman Rhee. The American troops began to slowly withdraw.

Both governments discredited the other. There were several conflicts between the militaries of each country, so tensions were running high. On January 17, 1950, North Korean leader Kim Il-Sung proposed the "liberation" of South Korea to Russian leaders. After weeks of exchanging telegrams, Russian Communist leader Joseph Stalin and Chinese Communist leader Mao Zedong approved the invasion of South Korea and agreed to provide military support, if necessary.

On June 25, 1950, roughly one hundred thousand North Korean troops invaded South Korea. It was obvious by the initial outcome that the South Korean military was not up to the task of defending its nation. However, to its credit, the South Korean military was driven back but not defeated.

United States president Truman had previously indicated that he would not use American troops to support South Korea. Instead, he appealed to the United Nations, who then called upon member nations to provide military assistance to South Korea.

The Soviet Union could have vetoed the resolution, Res. No. 83, but they were absent during the vote. They were protesting the fact that China's seat at the UN was held by a National Chinese representative, not a Communist one.

On June 28, the capital city of Seoul was captured by the North. The UN demanded the immediate removal of all North Korean troops from South Korea. North Korea ignored the UN. U.S. Army general Douglas MacArthur was appointed the supreme commander of UN Forces. MacArthur then deployed Task Force Smith from Japan to South Korea. Task Force Smith consisted of U.S. Army officers and regiments of the army's Twenty-Fourth Infantry Division. Undertrained, poorly supplied, and outnumbered, the Twenty-Fourth offered very little resistance against the North Korean advance. The army's Twenty-Fifth Infantry Division was deployed to Taejon, and the Twenty-Fourth ID was pulled out. But the North Korean advance continued.

By September 12, 1950, North Korean troops reached the farthest point of their advance. Thousands of UN troops arrived to reinforce South Korea. The best they could do was to set up a defensive barrier around the critical southeastern port of Pusan. By the time the North Korean invasion force reached the "Pusan perimeter," it was literally half of its starting size. It had lost almost all its armor.

Basically, the North Koreans had outdistanced their supply line, much like Germany in WWII when executing it "blitzkriegs."

While the main North Korean force was dashing toward Puran, General MacArthur persuaded President Truman of a daring plan that probably had odds of 5000:1 against it succeeding. But at this point it was worth a try. So on September 15, 1950, X Corps troops were landed 150 miles behind enemy lines at Incheon. The supply lines to the North Korean army in the South were cut, and Seoul was liberated ten days after the amphibious landing.

As I think about the importance of the supply chain to sustain combat, I have a whole new understanding of the critical nature of my mission in CBI. I knew it was extremely dangerous flying, but now I understand how necessary it was for the soldiers and sailors and airmen to have fuel, food, ammunition, weapons, clothing, and spare parts—things that we take for granted in peace time—when they need it.

By October 25, the bulk of the North Korean army had been destroyed. UN troops then pushed into North Korea and were nearing the Yalu River. The Yalu River formed the boundary between China and North Korea. Waiting on the other side of the Yalu River were tens of thousands of Chinese soldiers. The Chinese crossed the river and drove the UN forces back toward South Korea.

On December 6, 1950, the First Marine Division at the Chosin Reservoir was attacked by a huge Chinese force. Two entire Chinese armies had been tasked with the destruction of the First Marine Division consisting of ten to fifteen thousand soldiers. The Chinese were successful in driving the marines out of North Korea, but it cost them eight thousand killed or wounded.

On January 4, 1951, the Chinese and North Korean forces retook Seoul. On March 14, UN forces again liberated Seoul. The city was almost in ruins, and most of the people had evacuated.

On April 11, 1951, President Truman relieved Gen. Douglas MacArthur for insubordination. MacArthur was unwilling to prosecute a limited war. Lt. Gen. Matthew Ridgeway replaced General MacArthur.

April 1951 was a month of incredible heroism by a number of units who stood their ground against overwhelming numbers of Chinese. Two Commonwealth battalions, the Second Battalion of the Princess Patricia's Canadian Light Infantry Regiment and the Third Battalion of the Royal Australian Regiment, held off an entire Chinese division, which consists of between 12,000 and 20,000 soldiers. In addition, 4,000 men of the British Twenty-Ninth Brigade held off 30,000 troops of the Chinese Sixty-Third Army in a delaying action. And 650 men of the First Battalion Gloucestershire Regiment stood off more than 10,000 Chinese infantry. Most of the battalion were killed, but their bravery allowed UN forces to consolidate their lines around Seoul.

Peace talks began on July 10, 1951. Fighting continued for two more years while the negotiations dragged on.

Finally, on July 27, 1953, Gen. Mark W. Clark representing the UN Command, Peng Dehuai representing the Chinese, and Kim

Il-Sung representing North Korea concluded an armistice ending the hostilities. The armistice led to the establishment of a demilitarized zone that roughly followed the Thirty-Eighth parallel. Although Syngman Rhee announced his acceptance of the agreement, the agreement was not signed by him or any other representative of South Korea.

WHAT I LEARNED AFTER I ARRIVED IN JAPAN

The Command and Control Organization for the USAF forces in the Far East was the Far East Air Forces, Fifth Air Force. It had units in Korea and Japan. However, the air force, with its concept of major commands organized by function: Strategic Air Command, Tactical Air Command, Air Defense Command, etc. Money and development, I think, was focused more on the strategic combat, thanks to the effect of the atomic bomb. The mission of that command was hit an enemy's homeland with overwhelming force and create a desire for the end of hostilities. While that could work fine for all-out, declared war between nations, Korea was different. It was a limited war.

Now instead of the Strategic Air Command saving the day, we found ourselves with an air force ill-equipped in terms of a viable war plan. The best the B-29 could do was flatten cities. Fighting a tactical, in-the-trenches-type war was not what we had prepared for.

Of course, fighters and light bombers could perform interdiction strikes. However, I think most of them were already in storage at Davis-Monthan AFB in Arizona. In Korea, fighter and troop transport assets from the Tactical Air Command, along with Air National Guard units from the States, got involved.

The tactical units with their F-84s and F-51Ds conducted interdiction strikes on supply lines, attacked dams that irrigated North Korea's rice crops, and flew missions in close support of United Nations ground forces. AT-6 "Mosquitoes," amazingly versatile trainers, were used as forward air controllers. They provided communication links between ground troops and supporting aircraft. They also marked targets with smoke for easy identification by tactical strike aircraft. In addition, they could carry one thousand pounds of bombs and two .30-caliber machine guns. The AT-6 was an asset of the U.S. 6147th Tactical Control Squadron, which operated with the call-sign "Mosquito." The "Mosquito" nickname became associated with both the 6147th TCS and with their T-6 aircraft.[123]

A few groups of Strategic Air Command aging B-29 Superfortress bombers that were not part of the nuclear strike force were released for combat over the skies of Korea. Many of these B-29s were war-weary and brought out of five years of storage. The one mission flown in South Korea again North Korean troops was totally ineffective. After that, they were used only against strategic and large military targets in the North. The B-29s were based on Okinawa. The bases on the peninsula, as best I can remember, were the following:

Kunsan Air Base (K-8): No aircraft at beginning of invasion. After April 1, 1951, F-84s; B-26 invader. Location: on west coast, 110 miles south of Seoul.

Osan Air Base (K-55): Construction completed, and first squadron of F-51D Mustang received the day after Christmas in 1952. Other two squadrons arrived just after the New Year, and all squadrons converted to F-86F Sabre. Location: 64 miles south of Seoul.

Suwan Air Base (K-13): The base was captured twice, once in the original invasion by the North Koreans and the second time by the Chinese in January 1951. By January 28, the base was recaptured by the United States, and by March 6, the base was launching F-86 patrols along the Yalu River up to the area known as Mig Alley. Location: near Suwon City, about 20 miles south of Seoul.

Kimpo Air Base (K-14): I believe that this airport was used early on for evacuation of Seoul. Location: far west end of Seoul.

Yokota Air Base in Japan also played a major role. The base hosted F-82F/G aircraft, Twin Mustangs, which flew missions over South Korea during the first few months of the war. They also had the Fighter-Interceptor, the F-80C for Air Defense. Also hosted there were F–84Es in November and December 1950. These were used for fighter escort, reconnaissance, interdiction, and close air support for ground troops. B–29Ms, air tankers, were based there also.

The evacuation of U.S. citizens from Seoul was an amazing operation that had very little notice. SB–17s provided rescue cover for the initial evacuation, which was done by sea. Initial boarding of a Norwegian merchant ship began early in the morning. A total of 682 people boarded the "rescue" ship at Inchon Harbor. The ship left harbor about four thirty in the afternoon with an air escort of F–82G Twin Mustang fighters of the Sixty-Eighth Fighter All-Weather Squadron.

The Far East Air Forces used Suwon Air Field just twenty miles south of Seoul for air evacuation. C–54s, C–47s, and C–46s were used to evacuate 748 people from Seoul to Japan. The cargo aircraft were escorted by F–82s, F–80s, and B–26 light bombers.[124]

Some of the flying units had to move several times to different bases because of the ever-changing battle line.

Like the rest of the American military establishment, the air force was not really prepared for battle at the western rim of the Pacific. Yet despite these limitations, the air force responded quickly and effectively, proving in many ways the utility of airpower in modern war. With virtually no warning, the air force injected itself into the war in the first critical week. It transported troops and equipment from Japan to Korea, evacuated American nationals, provided significant intelligence through aerial reconnaissance, and most importantly, helped slow the North Korean advance so that the United Nations forces could construct a defensive position on the peninsula.

After about eighteen months, around November 1951, the fighting was still going on in Korea. I asked if they could tell me how much longer I would be there. After some time waiting for an answer, I was finally told that my tour had been for eighteen months. So I said, "Oh good! I want to go home." They replied, "Well, sorry old boy, but we have people here who were here when this thing first started. They've been here more than three years. So they will be going home first. Then we'll let you go home."

"Well, okay. About how long will that be?" I asked. "Oh, a couple of months," they replied. Those couple of months turned into another eight months before I was finally allowed to go home. Twenty-six months I had been in Japan without my family.

★ ★ ★ ★ ★

THE CLOUDS BEFORE THE KOREAN WAR

Stalin had been asked to declare war on Japan. The United States had not expected the Soviets to actually join the fight. The move was intended to intimidate Japan into surrendering in order to prevent an invasion of their homeland by the Soviets as well as the other Allies. Stalin seized the opportunity to invade Manchuria and reclaim territory that Russia had lost in previous wars with Japan. He also invaded Korea knowing that he would have a strong bargaining position for continued occupation when the war ended. His troops advanced as far as the Thirty-Eighth parallel. He would have gone farther if the war had lasted a few more weeks. Stalin showed his true colors as an opportunist rather than an ally.

Stalin had no intention of helping North Korea establish a representative government and then allowing the North Korean government and the South Korean government to have free elections in which all Koreans could select one government for all.

The United States naively withdrew large numbers of forces while the Soviet Union maintained a powerful presence in the north. According to the agreement on the disposition of Korea, both the United States and the Soviet Union were to remove their militaries and yield to the authority of the United Nations over the area. Only the United States withdrew.

The United States did not want to continue what had been World War II into what might become another war with the Soviet Union.

The United States was weary of war and trusted the Soviet Union to honor the authority of the United Nations.

Even before negotiations between North and South Korea broke down, the Soviet Union had built up a very strong North Korean military and supplied them with Soviet military hardware. The United States watched the military build-up in the north but chose to remain uninvolved. The South Korean military remained weak, poorly trained, and poorly equipped.

When the north eventually invaded the south, the "isolationist" United States addressed the United Nations. It was two days before the United Nations took action to condemn the invasion. The condemnation passed only because the Soviet Union, who could have vetoed the resolution, was absent at the vote. During the two days of hearings in the United Nations, the North Koreans had occupied almost all of South Korea.

After ignoring all of the signs of the upcoming conflict, the "clouds", South Korea was almost non-existent and their only means of salvation was a resolution by the United Nations that resulted in another war. The United States had essentially turned a blind eye to all the warning signs of a coming conflict until it was too late to prevent a war in order to preserve South Korea. That lack of action almost resulted in the elimination of South Korea.

One last sign, a towering cumulo-nimbus cloud of war on the horizon, was neighboring China. They were Communists. North Korea was Communist. It was incredibly naïve of General MacArthur to think that China would not come to the aid of North Korea.

★ ★ ★ ★ ★

A Cloud with a Silver Lining

Before I went home, though, my roommate, a black man, and I had become good friends. We were lodged in a hotel suite. We had a living room and a couple of bedrooms. He was in programs and plans, which included base housing. He was the base housing officer and had a master's degree. The master's degree had helped him edge out several other officers without master's degrees for his job as base housing officer.

One day, as my roommate and I were talking, he said, "Did you say that you didn't finish college?" I answered, "Yeah, I still have twenty-two hours to go." So he said, "Well, do you know about Operation Bootstrap?" I said, "No, I've never heard of it." He said, "Well, I'll tell you what. You can apply for it, and if you can complete your education, your twenty-two hours in six months, and the university you want to go to will accept you, the air force will let you go to school during your duty day and still pay in full." So I applied for it while I was over there. I knew I could get six hours in the summer session and pick up the other sixteen hours in one regular semester.

While I was still waiting to hear about my application, I was reassigned to Randolph AFB near San Antonio, Texas, as a supply officer.

Goodbye, Japan!

★ ★ ★ ★ ★

CHAPTER 17

Back in the States

BACK IN THE STATES

S O BACK IN the States, I moved my family—my wife, two boys, and daughter, Deborah, who had been born while I was in Japan—to San Antonio. We signed a rental agreement for a house in a little town called Schertz, Texas. It was about a mile from Randolph.

I reported to the base supply office at Randolph. About a week after I reported in, base personnel told me they had received a letter saying, "Send that kid back to college."

So we contacted Mary Lou's mom and discussed the logistics of our move back to Kansas City. She graciously agreed to come to Schertz and live in our house. Mary Lou and the children and I went back to Kansas City and occupied her house. That worked out very nicely, especially since her house was only one block from the St. Benedict's College.

The air force was going to cover all my pay and allowances for the six months of additional college but not the cost of travel, books, or tuition. So I checked with the Veterans Administration (VA) to see if I had enough left on the GI Bill to cover my books and tuition.

The nice folks at the VA said that I did have benefits left and that they would be happy to oblige.

So we moved back to Kansas City, and I enrolled at the University of Missouri in Kansas City. I signed up for the summer and fall semesters. My major was in economics, so the university required me to take two economics courses, one from a conservative economist and one from a liberal economist. One day as class was ending, the professor asked me to stay a few minutes after. This was the liberal professor. He asked me to consider going to another university to complete my program. I asked around about the university he mentioned and was told that it was very liberal and Leftist. It crossed my mind that maybe the Communists were shifting their strategy back to flooding the liberal universities with Communist professors and then funneling students into those universities for "reorientation." I was aware of a new alert on the Communist insurgency program, but I never expected to be approached by a recruiter. Gaining control of the educational content in U.S. schools was expressed in goals 17, 18, and 19 of the list of Communist goals, their insurgency plan, which would be read into the *Congressional Record* in 1963. I declined to commit to the professor. I completed school in January and graduated in May.

So back to San Antonio we went, degree in hand. I went to the personnel office at Randolph and said, "Hey, guys, I just got my degree in economics, and I'd like to have a position more aligned with economics than supply. I know supply falls into that category, but there are other jobs that I might like." They replied, "We have a job over at headquarters. Lt. Col. Paul Henslee, the director of management analysis, Office of the Comptroller, Crew Training Air Force on the base, has a position open in the management analysis office. I'll set up an interview for you tomorrow at one o'clock."

The next day, I went over to see Colonel Hensley at one o'clock. He started talking, and then we were talking, and finally, we broke up at five o'clock. When I left, he told me to report to his office in the morning, and he would take care of the paperwork to transfer me from base supply over to Crew Training Air Force (CTAF).

So I went to work for Paul in management analysis in the comptroller's office. Paul was a very intelligent man and a prince of a guy to work for. The mission of management analysis was to develop a monthly analysis report and then brief the CTAF commander on the report. We weren't too popular with the rest of the staff because, at times, the briefings brought out some problems that they had to explain.

In 1953, our lives changed significantly. Our third son, fourth child, Daniel, was born on April 1—no joke! Also, I received a regular commission and was also promoted to major. On October 9, 1954, our daughter Miriam came along. That made five children.

WAR IN THE TRENCHES

During my assignment to Crew TNG AF, I was also selected to participate in a nuclear test at a site in Nevada. I firmly believe I had made an enemy in AF personnel somewhere along my career, and that "enemy" wanted to blow me off the face of the planet!

I was flown to the site where a group of us were placed in a trench a few thousand yards[125] away from ground zero. There was an atomic device on top of a tower and many trenches in the area where we were. We were told to get into the trenches, turn our backs to the tower, and kneel. We were told not to stand until after the second whistle blew. The reason for this was to avoid being covered with radioactive dust. After the bomb explodes, a cloud of radioactive dust passed over the ground and then reversed direction.

After the second whistle, we exited the trenches and walked within about a mile of ground zero and examined the damage done to vehicles, tanks, etc.

I still get letters from the Defense Department asking about my physical condition. At age ninety-six, it seems to be a waste of a stamp!

I've recently learned that the shot was named APPLE I.

Operation Teapot

Nuclear Tests – February 18–June 10, 1955

Teapot Apple I (Courtesy: Los Alamos National Labs)

APPLE I, a shot from a 500-foot tower detonation, was fired at 4:55 a.m. on March 29, 1955. Its yield was 14 kilotons. The shot was carried out in Area 4 of Yucca Flat.

The more than six hundred troops observing the shot were exposed to fallout of up to 10 R/h. Troops witnessed the detonation from trenches 3,200 meters (2 miles) from ground zero.

After the detonation, the troops left the trenches and toured the equipment area at 900 to 2,250 meters (0.56 to 1.4 miles) from ground zero.

In another Exercise Desert Rock project, about twenty-four persons conducted surveys of the ground zero area on the day after the shot.[126]

This was a Los Alamos Science Labs test of a Class "D" (lightweight) thermonuclear weapon primary and radiation implosion system. Small quantities of fusion fuel were used. The primary fuse failed, yielding much less than the predicted 40 kt. No reaction was detected in the secondary stage. The nuclear system was 29.5 inches wide and 74.6 inches long and weighed 2,300 pounds.[127]

END OF WAR IN THE TRENCHES

Also in 1955, we acquired a new comptroller, Col. Shirley Black. He had been the director of management analysis at headquarters training command. Paul was reassigned to Laughlin AFB in Del Rio, Texas, as the base comptroller. Colonel Black appointed me to replace Paul as the director of management analysis.

One day in June 1956, Colonel Black called me into his office and introduced me to a Lt. Col. Bill Donnley from AFIT (Air Force Institute of Technology). Colonel Donnley asked me if I would like to go to AFIT and get an MBA degree (masters in business administration). Naturally, I didn't have to be asked twice.

It seems that General Ancencio, comptroller of the air force, felt that all air force comptrollers should have an MBA and was establishing the program at AFIT. The criteria was that you had to be at least a major or above and have a bachelor's degree in economics, mathematics, or a related field. Out of all the officers in the AF comptroller field that year, only twenty-three met the criteria or chose to participate in the program. Actually, of the twenty-three in the first class, only fifteen of us qualified as candidates for the degree. The other eight had hours in the required fields but did not have the required undergraduate degree. At the end of the course, they received credit hours for the courses taken.

I always wondered what justification the general used for establishing the program. My guess was that it had something to do with the Nation Security Act of 1947. In addition to restructuring our military, the act provided for the creation of an office of the comptroller. All appropriated funds for the military would move through and be accounted for by this office.

The act created a National Security Council consisting of the president, vice president, secretary of state, secretary of defense, and other members, such as the director of the Central Intelligence Agency. They met at the White House to discuss long-term and short-term problems and also problems that represented more immediate national security crises.

JERRY L. BURTON

The War Department and Navy Department were merged into a single Department of Defense. The Department of the Air Force was created largely from the Army Air Corps. These three departs operated under the secretary of defense. Each of the three branches maintained their own service secretaries. In 1949, the act was amended to give the secretary of defense more control over the each service and their respective secretaries.[128]

So in August, we moved again. This time we went to Wright-Patterson AFB near Dayton, Ohio, and I became a member of the first comptroller course at AFIT.

The duration of the course was a little over one year. We went to classes six days a week except at the end of a quarter. Then we would attend class through the weekend. At the age of thirty-two, Maj. Bill Nugent and I were the youngest in the classroom. The oldest "student" was a major around the age of forty-four.

One afternoon, four of us were walking around the class building, Bldg. 125. Professor Lazar from our program asked if any of us would be interested in volunteering for a program after we graduated.

We asked all the logical questions, like what would we be doing, where would we be located, etc. The answer to all our questions was "Sorry, that's classified." We all held "top secret" clearances. Of course, our response to him was "Negative. Not interested." To this day, I don't know what it was that he wanted us to volunteer for! I sometimes wonder if it had anything to do with the space program and NASA that was gearing up at the time.

In March 1957, while still at AFIT, our youngest daughter, Martha, was born at the base hospital. That rounded out the "half dozen."

Then at the end of the classes, I graduated!

★ ★ ★ ★ ★

CHAPTER 18

Post–AFIT Assignments

M Y FIRST ASSIGNMENT out of school had the potential to be an excellent kickoff for me as a young major with an MBA and a lot of experience. The position comptroller for the Sixty-Third Troop Carrier Wing at Donaldson AFB in Greenville, South Carolina. The unit had C-124s at the time.

When I reported for duty, I was told by the personnel officer that they already had a comptroller. I explained that I had been told that the previous comptroller had left, and I had been assigned to the slot.

The personnel officer acknowledged that the previous comptroller had left but that a lieutenant colonel in another organization whose unit was relocating had wanted to stay at Donaldson. So he filled the slot with the lieutenant colonel.

Then I was told that I would have to be the lieutenant colonel's deputy.

I asked, "Is he a comptroller?" He answered, "No. But he can be made into one."

I obviously was not happy about it, but I had already moved my family to Greenville, so I stayed.

After I had been there about eight or nine months, MAC headquarters sent down an IG team, and the director of budget for MAC was the comptroller representative on the team. He asked me what I was doing, and I said, "Nothing!"

"What are you talking about nothing?" he asked.

So I told him the story.

He replied, "Oh no!" Then he said, "We'll fix that!"

The team finished their inspection and went back to MAC headquarters. Less than a week later, I had orders reassigning me to headquarters MAC at Scott AFB, Illinois, in the management analysis office.

I moved to Scott AFB in April 1958. On July 1, AMC (Air Mobility Command) was going to start the industrial fund concept within AMC. When I got there, the comptroller called me into his office and explained, "Our whole system is changing. On July 1, we will begin operating under an industrial fund concept."

He explained the new system to me as follows.

Individual military units requesting movement of personnel or cargo by airlift will submit their manifests to the comptroller at their respective AMC base. Each base comptroller will cost out the manifest and send it, via AMC Data Services, to AMC headquarters. Headquarters will service the information against the corpus of about $73 million.

At the end of the three months of operation, the total of manifest information collected would be reconciled to the balance of the corpus. Theoretically, the sum of the two should be $73 million. If we need more or less money, then the corpus will be adjusted at that time."

One day the comptroller called me in and said, "The problem I see with this process is there's a lag of anywhere from a few days to several weeks before we get our data. I need the data in a timely manner. So here's what I want you to do. I want you to prepare a daily report and have it on my board every day on my wallboard, in my office, from each of our bases, as to how much traffic is going in and out of that base—how much we hauled. Get the information from operations, cost it out unofficially, then put it on my board. Then let the official costs come through the other way."

As the end of the three-month period drew near, the comptroller called me in and declared, "We're going to be about $3 million short!"

I responded, "Well, sir, not according to my figures. I've got the manifests, and according to my figures, we may be down $100,000 or something like that, but we're not any $3 million short."

He said, "I appreciate your effort, but I have to go by what has been officially reported."

At the end of the three months, we went to Department of Defense. They approved our figures and gave us more money.

I understand that several months after I had left MAC, an IG team was asking questions about the industrial fund system and how it was working at the operational level.

Most of the answers were positive, but there was some concern about the manifests the team had found at several bases. The manifests were just sitting in a drawer of the base comptrollers' desks.

They didn't know how to cost them, so we didn't send them in. Guess what they totaled. Yes, close to $3 million!

★ ★ ★ ★ ★

Command and Staff What?

Now here's one place that I messed up. I had never been to Command and Staff College. General De Laney had an open position on staff and sent his adjutant to me. The adjutant said, "The general would like to see you go to Command and Staff College." I replied, "Well, I don't know, but from a technical point of view, we were told that with an MBA, we didn't have to go to Command and Staff College."

I went home and told Mary Lou about it, and she said, "Not only no, but NO! You've been gone enough, and you need to stay home for a while."

I told General De Laney, "I don't think it is in my best interest to go at this point in time." He said, "I think I understand."

BACK TO JAPAN

Later on, I received orders to the Far East. My brother Bob, also in the air force, was at Hickam AFB in Hawaii. He sent me a message to inform me that there was an opening for a comptroller there. He asked me if I would like to consider that slot. I, of course, said yes. Before I could get over to apply for it, the slot was canceled. That left me on orders going to the Far East!

So I received my assignment, and it was to headquarters NAMAP, headquarters at Tachikawa Air Base in the western part of the Tokyo area.

We went by ship to Japan with a stop in Hawaii, where we visited with friends before continuing to Japan. I was the ranking air force officer on the ship; therefore, I was commander of all the air force personnel on board—wife, mother-in-law, our children, and an air force chaplain. That was it!

Somewhere between Hawaii and Japan, the ship conducted a "man overboard" (MOB) drill. We were all standing at the rail watching.

In the drill, someone yelled, "Man overboard!" That person continued to watch the person who went into the water. Keeping a "visual" on the person is critical. As soon as the MOB cry was heard, a buoy or "lifesaver" was thrown into the water to provide a visual location marker. The bridge was immediately made aware of the MOB so that the navigator could mark his location and the helmsman could begin maneuvering the ship in a "search and recovery" pattern. If there are other vessels in the area, they might offer assistance. There might or might not have been a floating smoke device dropped into the water when the buoy was deployed.

When the MOB is sighted, the ship or rescue vessel, if one is launched, is maneuvered toward the MOB. In the case of the drill we watched, when the "pickup man" was close enough to the MOB dummy, he took a long pole with a hook on the end and viciously stabbed the dummy in the chest and pulled him in! Some people were shocked. My children thought it was hilarious! The "takeaway" for them was, if you fall overboard, you're going to die either from drowning or from a sharp stab in the chest! But either way, you're dead!

After about a week, we arrived in port at Tokyo. It took three taxis to transport all of us and our baggage to Tachikawa!

The boys went to St. Mary's International School, and Deborah and Miriam went to the Madams of the Sacred Heart in Tokyo. Martha went to a nearby Japanese school. None of the other children or teachers in the school spoke English. Mary Lou and I took classes learning about the culture and how to speak Japanese.

Brother John at the boys' school heard that I had played high school basketball. He asked me to coach the St. Mary's junior school basketball team. Naturally, I said I would. We won the championship trophy for all the military schools in the area. Brother John, of course, was ecstatic.

The Materiel Air Command was undergoing some drastic changes in structure in the Far East at the time I was assigned there. Northern Area Materiel Air Pacific (NAMAP) and Southern Area Materiel Air Support (SAMAP) were being closed down.

When the Vietnam War began, we were using C-141s to supply directly from the States to the bases. Everything was computerized.

So consequently, it closed down NAMAP and SAMAP. I was moved then to the 315th Air Division at Tachikawa. Gen. Theodore Kershaw was the commander. They had a slot for a comptroller, so I went over there as a comptroller. There was a whole lot of work

JERRY L. BURTON

to do, and I was doing a real good job. I had a fine relationship with the deputy commander and general Kershaw and everybody else in the command.

One day General Kershaw called me in and said, "I have a request here. It's from Fuchu Headquarters from the comptroller. He would like to have you assigned at Fifth Air Force Management Analysis." I quickly responded, "Who made the request?" General Kershaw answered, "Colonel Black." Colonel Black had made it possible for me to go to AFIT to get my MBA. General Kershaw said, "If you want to stay here, it will be fine, but if you feel you need to go, I understand."

I told the general that I pretty much felt an obligation to Colonel Black because of what he had done for me in the past. So I transferred to management analysis at Fifth Air Force.

When I got there, I thought I was going to be the management analysis officer, but there was a lieutenant colonel who was already in that job. It turned out that my friend Colonel Black was very involved with Little League Baseball, and he wanted me to be the commissioner of Little League Baseball in Japan!

I stayed with Colonel Black until my tour was up. After that, my family and I went back to the States, and I was assigned to the director of management analysis at headquarters USAF in Washington, DC.

★ ★ ★ ★ ★

BACK TO THE STATES

We returned to the States via Seattle. Mary Lou took the two youngest girls, Miriam and Martha, and flew on to Baltimore to pick up our car and drive it to Washington. The others had never been on a train. So we got a train out of Seattle to Chicago so we could see my aunt Sadie. From there, we went on to Washington, DC.

Somewhere along the trip, I think around Chicago, I developed a sore in the calf of my right leg. By the time we got to Washington, I was just hobbling along. Mary Lou met us at the station and said, "I have some houses lined up." So we and the kids went out to look at houses. While we were out, Martha got stung by a bee. Fort Belvoir was the closest hospital in the area, so we went there and saw the doctor at emergency. The doctor took care of Martha, but in the course of things, Mary Lou asked the doctor to look at my leg and told him that I'd had this "charley horse" for the last week.

The doctor looked at it, called the nurse, and told her to get a gurney. When the gurney arrived, he said, "Get up there." I got onto the gurney and went from the gurney to the bed and was in the bed for three weeks. The doctor told me that I had a blood clot!

Poor Mary Lou was saddled with looking for a house. She finally found one out in Vienna, Virginia, and got all the paperwork lined up. Getting the paperwork signed was a real trick because she was back and forth getting signatures while I was still in the hospital.

The doctor put me on Coumadin, and I finally got to work. I worked in the Pentagon for four years. That was the worst assignment I ever had. In fact, it was worse than the twenty-six-month isolated tour in Japan during the Korean War. The cost of living was prohibitive. To obtain adequate living quarters for the family, we had to buy a home in Vienna, Virginia, a three-hour round-trip drive to the Pentagon.

The Cuban Missile Crisis

Remember the Cuban Missile Crisis? I was in the Pentagon at the time. My boss was a GS-15. I remember him informing us of the Defense Readiness Condition (Defense Readiness Condition) dropping from 5 (no immediate threat) to 4, and then 3, and then 2, and ultimately, it got down to 1, according to him. As you can see from the table I've constructed below, 1 means "maximum readiness; nuclear war is imminent."

Readiness condition	Exercise term	Description	Readiness
DEFCON 1	COCKED PISTOL	Nuclear war is imminent	Maximum readiness
DEFCON 2	FAST PACE	Next step to nuclear war	Armed Forces ready to deploy and engage in less than six hours
DEFCON 3	ROUND HOUSE	Increase in force readiness above that required for normal readiness	Air force ready to mobilize in fifteen minutes
DEFCON 4	DOUBLE TAKE	Increased intelligence watch and strengthened security measures	Above normal readiness
DEFCON 5	FADE OUT	Lowest state of readiness	Normal readiness

My family and I lived in Vienna, which was west of Washington. So I went to the GS-15 and asked him, "What's the evacuation plan?"

To my surprise, he replied, "Evacuation plan? There isn't one. We're all expendable."

I responded, "Theoretically, the best minds in the military and other government agencies are here in Washington, and you're telling me there is no evacuation plan in case?"

"That's right," he replied.

I thought for a moment and then said, "Is that right? Well, that's strange. What do you think we should do?"

He replied, "Just stay here and get blown up."

I said, "You got to be kidding me! I've never heard anything so dumb in all my life!"

Here we were, in DEFCON-1, so I called Mary Lou. We had a Dodge Caravan that seated eight people. So I told Mary Lou, "Get food and clothing packed into the van, and if I call you, get the kids into that van and head west just as fast as you can go and as far as you can go. I'll try to get a call to you somewhere along the line, or you call me, if possible. She understood.

It just seemed unwise to me to have so many people involved in such a limited space, to pay them all that money, to value them so highly on the one hand, and then to refer to them as expendable on the other. Isn't that contradictory?

Besides that, from what I was able to observe, the majority of personnel in the Pentagon would be more effective and productive if assigned to their counterparts in the field. The whole system would certainly be less vulnerable.

As most people know, our navy turned the Soviet ships around and sent them back.

Fog of War: Here are some details that many people may not know:

1. U.S. Deployment of Tactical Nuclear Weapons (TNW):[129]
   - In 1953, the United States began deploying tactical (short range or less-than-201-mile range) missiles throughout Europe, beginning with Great Britain.
   - During the Cold War, Greece, the UK, Belgium, Germany, Italy, the Netherlands, Turkey, and the United States.
   - At the peak of the Cold War in the 1960s, these tactical nuclear weapons (TNW) numbered about seven thousand.

2. The Missiles in Italy and Turkey:[130]
   - The United States, in 1959, completed negotiations with Italy and Turkey that would allow the placement of thirty SM-78 missiles in Italy and fifteen SM-78 missiles in Turkey.
   - The squadrons in Italy and Turkey became operational in June and November 1961, respectively.
   - At the time the SM-78s were placed in Italy and Turkey, the United States knew they would be short-lived. The

navy would be replacing these SM–78s with their new submarine-launched ballistic missile by June 1963.

3. What led up to the Cuban Missile Crisis:
    *   Fidel Castro seized power in January 1959. He sought acceptance from the United States but was rejected by the Eisenhower administration. A year later, he aligned himself with the Soviet Union.
    *   On April 17, 1961, 1,400 Cuban exiles were captured, invading Cuba to overthrow Fidel Castro. The air support that was promised them was canceled by Pres. John F. Kennedy, who got cold feet and was concerned about domestic criticism and Soviet retaliation.
    *   After the Vienna Summit in June 1961, Khrushchev characterized the president as "weak and immature."[131]
    *   Berlin Crisis, in August 1961, led to the construction of a wall between East and West Berlin. Khrushchev wasn't deterred at all by President Kennedy. With the wall came heightened tensions in the Cold War.

4. The stalemate and the resolution:
    *   The initiatives for breaking the stalemate and keeping the peace came primarily from Khrushchev, who appealed to President Kennedy to "show statesmanlike wisdom."[132] Clearly, Khrushchev could sense that President Kennedy was unable to think his way through this problem. In fact, Robert Kennedy, working through the Soviet ambassador to the United States Anatoly Dobrynin did more to resolve the conflict than did President Kennedy, who was paralyzed by fear of over the legacy he might leave.[133]
    *   The resolution of this crisis was suggested by Khrushchev, who correctly feared that the young president would not be able to offer a peaceful solution. Khrushchev knew that the SM–78 Jupiter missiles in Turkey would be

removed in eight months because of obsolescence. The Polaris SLBM would be online. Khrushchev was the man who thought the situation through, looked at it from many angles, and came up with a solution. And even then, President Kennedy missed it. Luckily, Robert was on the same page with Khrushchev.

- The final agreement was that Khrushchev would publicly announce that he had ordered his ships to turn around and that a deal had been worked out for the removal of the missiles from Cuba. Khrushchev also agreed to keep the part about the United States, removing its missiles from Turkey a secret. This was a stipulation placed on the agreement by President Kennedy himself. Again, he was concerned about the political damage it would do to the United States in the eyes of its Allies and the personal political damage it would do him. So they all agreed to not tell the people of the United States or anyone in the free world.[134]

- Nikita S. Khrushchev probably saved the world from a nuclear holocaust and a young American president from a political fall by agreeing, in October 1962, to keep the American "concession" a secret. He, of course, could not keep that secret from his own government. The secret he kept made the United States look strong and the Soviet Union look weak as if it had backed down. In October 1964, Khrushchev was recalled from vacation and removed from his position as Soviet premier.[135]

- It may be that his peers in the Soviet Union, while rejecting him as premier, admired, to some degree, how hard he had worked to keep an inexperienced, frightened young man from starting World War III. Khrushchev was allowed to live out his life until he died of a heart attack in 1971.

★ ★ ★ ★ ★

ALBUQUERQUE

In May or June 1966, as my tour was about to end at the Pentagon, I accessed a printout of all the comptrollers in the United States Air Force, where they were assigned, when they had gotten there, and when they were due to leave. Mary Lou felt so well with her sinuses when we were in Roswell that we thought New Mexico was where would like to retire.

Sure enough, I found a comptroller at the Defense Atomic Support Agency (DASA) Test & Evaluation Facility on Sandia Base, Albuquerque, New Mexico, who was due for reassignment in July, the same time I would be leaving the Pentagon. So I called him up on the phone, and I asked him, "Do you have that slot filled yet as far as you know?"

He said, "No. As far as I know, we don't." So I told him who I was and what I was doing. Then he said, "Why don't you come on out here and visit us and meet the Commander and we'll see what he thinks?"

I replied, "I don't have the money right now to go out there on my own."

"Don't worry about that," he said. "I'll send you a ticket. We have some travel funds for that purpose."

So he sent me a ticket, and I went to Albuquerque, New Mexico, for an interview and stayed in the BOQ. I met the commander and received briefings on the position. At that time, the commander was Air Force Colonel Perkett. When I left to go back to Washington, Colonel Perkett said, "On your way back, I'm going to request you for that assignment. When you get back up there, you put in for this position, and there shouldn't be any problem."

Sure enough, it worked out. We arrived in Albuquerque on July 4, 1966, and I reported on the Fifth. As temporary quarters, they gave us two sets of two-bedroom apartments on the base. We ended up with four bedrooms, two living rooms, two kitchens, etc. These apartments were in two-story barracks that had been converted to apartments. We were also issued dishes, pots, and pans; cots to sleep on; and yes, there were two sets of stairs, side by side to the second floor, with a wall in between.

We had some very nice neighbors, Bob and Jerie Bartusch, who also had six children. When we had a barbecue, we had our own little community picnic. We still stay in touch at Christmas. Bob and Jerie now live in Florida.

There was a world of difference between Albuquerque, New Mexico, and Vienna, Virginia. In Vienna, I was in a car pool, and it took an hour and a half just to get to my office. Three hours a day just traveling! In Albuquerque, I got quarters on the base, I got a parking space right in front of my house, and there were real nice people to work with. We had army, navy, air force, and marines all working in this one command and working on the same project. Best assignment I ever had!

Test command did all the nuclear weapons effects testing for the services in the Department of Defense. It was part of DASA, and personnel assigned were from the air force, navy, marines, and army. Of all the units I was assigned to during my time in the service, test command personnel were undoubtedly the most professional, competent, cooperative, and congenial. It was a pleasure to go to work!

The comptroller billet that I filled was air force. I reported directly to the deputy commander, a navy captain, Robert "Gus" Duborg. He was a prince of a guy. We became real good friends.

The first day I reported for work, I was sitting at my desk in my office, and Captain Duborg came walking into the office. I was reading something. He stood in front of me, and I looked up, and he said, "Do you play squash?"

I replied, "Squash what?" He just looked at me, and I felt like I probably said the wrong thing to him. He was a 6'2", 240-pound navy guy, and I thought, *Man, he's going to kill me for being a "smart aleck."*

Then he took a deep breath and responded, "Meet me at the gym at 11:30 a.m. I'm going to teach you the game." Since I was going to be working for him for the next three years, I thought I had better comply.

We became very good friends. So he taught me the game of squash, and handball, and racket ball. He beat the socks off me for the first six months, and then I started beating him because I was faster and lighter. One day when we were playing, he whacked me with a racket across the knuckles. It turned black and blue, and he said, "We better stop. You're going to the hospital and have them take a look at that. They might have to take an X-ray or something." And so I did. They looked at it and said it was a really bad bruise, but there was nothing to it.

The next day when I went in to work, he walked into my office and said, "Well, what did the folks at the hospital say?"

I replied, "Well, I didn't know what to tell them because they wanted to know how this accident happened so they could write up an accident report. So I just told them I was playing racket ball with my boss, and he got mad at me because—"

He interrupted, "You didn't!"

I answered, "Well, no, not really. At least not exactly in those words." Despite that, I got some real good OERs out of him. During my tour with test command, I was promoted to lieutenant colonel.

We developed an excellent work, athletic, and family relationship, which we enjoyed well into retirement. He even taught me to ski, something I had never done before.

★ ★ ★ ★ ★

RETIREMENT?

When it came time for my next assignment, I asked for an extension and then planned to retire. After a promotion, you had to serve two years in grade to retire at that grade. My good friends in air force personnel reminded me that I still had one year to go to fulfill my two years in grade. They suggested that, even though I had already served in two combat zones, World War II and Korea, I might be interested in serving in the conflict going on in Vietnam. It was a one-year tour and would satisfy my in-grade requirement.

Retirement? No. So off I went to Vietnam.

★ ★ ★ ★ ★

CHAPTER 19

The Vietnam War

FRENCH INDOCHINA[136]

THE REGION OF Vietnam, Laos, and Cambodia were once called French Indochina. The French had colonized the area during the late 1800s. They, of course, set up a French colonial government. The French were filling their coffers through taxes on consumer goods like salt, opium, and rice alcohol. The taxes paid to the French colonial government amounted to 44 percent of the government's entire budget by 1920.

In the 1930s, as the local population became too poor to pay the high taxes, the French began exploiting the natural resources such as zinc, tin, and coal and cash crops such as rice, rubber, coffee, and tea from the area now known as Vietnam. The area known as Cambodia was a good supply of rice, rubber, coffee, and tea. The area now known as Laos could only supply low-level timber. Michelin Tire Company was started by French investment dollars. The French invested in building factories in Vietnam for the production of cigarettes, alcohol, and textiles for export markets.

When World War II started, the Japanese invaded French Indochina. The Vichy French, Nazi allies, turned Indochina over to the

Japanese. Some Japanese military figures encouraged nationalism and independence. However, the higher military and government officials in Japan saw Indochina as a valuable source of natural resources.

Now instead of being mercilessly exploited by the French, they were being mercilessly exploited by the Japanese. This gave rise to a new nationalist group of guerilla fighters known as the League for the Independence of Vietnam, also known as the Viet Minh. The Viet Minh fought against Japanese occupation.

At the end of World War II, France expected to have Indochina returned to it. However, the Indochinese wanted independence. This led to the First Indochina War. Ho Chi Minh eventually defeated the French at the Battle of Dien Bien Phu. France then gave up their claim to rule in 1954.

HO CHI MINH[137]

Ho was born in what is now Vietnam. He grew up under French rule and Confucian culture. At the age of twenty-one, he took a job as a cook's helper on board a ship. This job took him to many port cities in countries, including Africa, Asia, and France. Along the way, he developed a dislike for French colonialists.

At some point, he stopped for a period in the United States. He worked as a baker's assistant in Boston at a large hotel—the Omni Parker House. He also spent time in New York City. What Ho observed was that Asians could do quite well for themselves in a freer environment than living under colonial rule.

In 1919, Ho went to Paris to the Paris Peace Conference to attempt to present his argument for independence from colonialism for Vietnam. Only the Communist and socialist parties were sympathetic to him. At that point, he became a Communist and began reading Marx.

Ho went to Russia for some training and then to China in 1924. There, he trained operatives and raised funds for strikes against French colonials in Southeast Asia. In 1927, Chiang Kai-shek, the Chinese leader, began purging Communists. Ho left China.

Ho moved around for about thirteen years and finally ended up back in Vietnam in 1941. The distraction of the Nazis defeat of France allowed him the opportunity to return to his country.

When the Japanese entered Vietnam, Ho and his guerilla fighters opposed them. When the Japanese left Vietnam in defeat, Ho quickly declared Vietnam's independence and also declared himself president. The name of this new Vietnam was the Democratic Republic of Vietnam.

Warring broke out between France and the Democratic Republic of Vietnam. It ended in 1949 in defeat for France. France pulled out of Indochina. Ho was given governing power over Northern Vietnam, and Ngo Dinh Diem, a capitalist leader in the south who was backed by the United States, was given governing power in Southern Vietnam. The Geneva Accords of 1954 had separated the north from the south at the seventeenth parallel and established demilitarized zones on each side. The two sides were hold an election in 1956 to determine how they would unify—whether under the Communist side or under the Nationalist side. The elections were canceled by the government in the south. The United States was supporting the south because the north was Communist, and the United States was operating under the principle of the "Domino Theory." This theory proposed that if one country falls to Communism, it will cause the fall of another country.

Now the stage was set for the Vietnam War.

However, there was an aspect of Ho's guerilla warfare that played a larger role in the Vietnam War that most people were aware of at the time.

THE CU CHI TUNNELS[138]

During the final decade of French rule in Vietnam, 1941–1949, there were tens of thousands of miles of underground tunnels dug throughout Northern and Southern Vietnam. They were dug to enable Vietnamese guerilla warriors to hit, run, and hide as they fought the French. These tunnels also were rest areas, living areas, hospitals, meeting and planning areas, and safe areas when hostile troops were in the area. There were storage rooms for food, clothing, weapons, munitions, and whatever else a soldier might need. Civilians and soldiers shared these areas.

The tunnels allowed mass movements of troops and supplies without the enemy being able to observe the movement. In the south, these tunnels were "home" to thousands of Viet Cong and Viet Cong sympathizers.

Entering a tunnel complex was extremely dangerous for an enemy. There were booby traps as well as natural hazards such as snakes and poisonous insects.

An area that was swept by a patrol might appear to be void of Viet Cong. Yet just under the feet of the patrol were a hundred armed Viet Cong or North Vietnamese Army.

I'm not sure the United States had any idea how extensive the tunnel networks were and what an important role they played during the war.

The War before I Got There

Ho Chi Minh organized a counter movement in the south to oppose the government of Diem. That counter movement became known as the Viet Cong.

The Diem government was not doing well, so President Kennedy, in 1962, sent American troops, acting as "advisors," to help train the South Vietnamese Army, ARVN.

Nothing really got better, so in 1963, the United States backed a coup that overthrew and replaced Diem. Nothing got better after the change.

On November 22, 1963, President Kennedy was assassinated. The intent of Pres. Lyndon B. Johnson was to keep the troop level in Vietnam to a minimum.

However, on August 2, 1964, North Vietnamese forces fired on the USS *Maddox* in the Gulf of Tonkin. President Johnson approached Congress, and Congress approved the use of whatever force was necessary to keep the situation under control.

That decision by Congress led to increase after increase in the number of American troops in Vietnam. By the end of 1966, the number of troops in Vietnam had risen to almost four hundred thousand.

The United States began a bombing campaign that would increase in its intensity and last almost three years. Operation Rolling Thunder finally came to an end on November 2, 1968.

★ ★ ★ ★ ★

THE LAY OF THE LAND

So in 1969, I once again found myself in a foreign conflict. I was assigned as the comptroller for the Thirty-Fifth Air Base Group at Phan Rang, Vietnam. It was the biggest fighter base in Vietnam.

The host unit on the base was the Thirty-Fifth Tac Fighter Wing flying F–100C/D/Fs (courtesy of USAF 600th Photo Sqdn – 1970).

The tenant units included the Fourteenth Special Operations Wing with the C–119 Flying Boxcars with the light in the back end.

By U.S. Air Force – Official U.S. Air Force photo 021001-O-9999G-016, Public Domain

Another tenant unit was the 315th Airlift Wing with C–123s.

C–123K at Phan Rang, Vietnam

A medical evacuation helicopter unit, the 247th Medical Detachment (helicopter ambulance) – Dustoff – was also stationed at Phan Rang.

In addition, we had an army artillery unit, the Fifth/Twenty-Seventh Field Artillery Unit stationed at Phan Rang. And finally, in one corner of the base, we had 2,800 South Koreans. We left them alone! Every morning, they would send a contingent out on a hunt-and-kill mission, and they would find these guys, kill them or whatever, and come back. They were doing their thing, and we just left them alone.

Anyway, it was a very large base. I technically worked for a group commander within the Thirty-Fifth Air Base Wing. He was a great guy! None of the other wings on the base brought a comptroller. They just brought their money and people and had an office. So I took care of everybody's pay and all that sort of stuff for the base commander.

Basically, I handled the finances for the whole base. While I was in Vietnam, I had a good relationship with the group commander, wing commander, and base commander. I was awarded the Bronze Star while I was over there. It was a good tour.

I only got to see Mary Lou one time while I was in Vietnam. After six months in Vietnam, I was allowed one R & R. You weren't allowed to come back to the conterminous United States. You were allowed, however, to go to Hawaii, the Philippines, Japan, or someplace like that.

★ ★ ★ ★ ★

JERRY L. BURTON

CHAPTER 20

Retirement

DURING MY TOUR in Vietnam, I put in for retirement when I returned to the United States. My request was returned as a function of the "seven-day rule." Apparently, the "rule" states that when a person applies for retirement, they must wait seven days and then decide whether to apply for a stateside tour at a location of their choice or actually retire. So I requested a comptroller position at Kirtland AFB, New Mexico, or comptroller of any other base in New Mexico or Arizona.

Personnel responded with comptroller of the Northern Communication Region, AMC, Griffiss AFB, New York. I had been to Griffiss AFB once before on an inspection trip while in AMC. My answer was an immediate no; I would rather retire. The weather was horrible there.

So I came back to Albuquerque and retired.

Gus, the navy captain, left here (AFOTEC) about the same time I did. He went to Europe as the navy representative of NATO or one of those joint commands over there. I believe he was over there for, I think, two years. Then he came back to Albuquerque, and he retired.

We got together again and played squash. One day he said to me, "Hey, don't you ski?" I said, "Ski? Never heard of it." We both had a good laugh.

The Officers' Wives Club here had a ski club, and we joined that. We skied with them for some time. In the wintertime, during the ski season, they set up six or seven trips to six places like Colorado. It was a really good deal. I haven't been able to ski, though, because of my legs for the last four or five years. So I dropped out of it.

I don't know how I got plagued with this phenomenon, but the two friendships I made in the service that carried over after retirement were both navy men.

Gus Duburg, his family, and my family maintained a close relationship until he passed on about four or five years ago. I miss him.

Bill Crane worked for me in the comptroller office and headed up the program and plans division. Bill was a navy lieutenant and stationed in Nha Trang during the Vietnam War. He was a Navy SEAL. He was married to a woman named Nancy. They both were from Colorado.

Bill and I liked to play golf. We did a lot of that when we were in the service, and after retiring, we added fishing. He, his dad, and his friends would go salmon and steel head fishing in Washington and Canada.

★ ★ ★ ★ ★

For the Record

I retired from the United States Air Force in 1970 as a lieutenant colonel.

My Medals Include Bronze Star

The Bronze Star Medal, unofficially the Bronze Star, is a United States decoration awarded to members of the United States Armed

Forces for either heroic achievement, heroic service, meritorious achievement, or meritorious service in a combat zone.

★ ★ ★ ★ ★

AIR MEDAL

The original award criteria set by an Army Policy Letter dated September 25, 1942, was for one award of the Air Medal: twenty-five operational flights during which exposure to enemy fire is expected.

★ ★ ★ ★ ★

AIR FORCE COMMENDATION MEDAL

The Air Force Commendation Medal may be awarded to members of the Armed Forces of the United States below the grade of brigadier general who, while serving in any capacity with the air force, distinguish themselves by heroism, outstanding achievement, or meritorious service not of a sufficient nature to justify a higher award.

★ ★ ★ ★ ★

ASIATIC-PACIFIC CAMPAIGN

The Asiatic–Pacific Campaign Medal is a United States military award of the Second World War that was awarded to any member of the United States Armed Forces who served in the Asiatic-Pacific Theater from 1941 to 1945.

★ ★ ★ ★ ★

Japanese Occupation

The Army of Occupation Medal is a military award of the United States military that was established by the United States War Department on April 5, 1946. The medal was created in the aftermath of the Second World War to recognize those who had performed occupation service in either Germany, Italy, Austria, or Japan. The original Army of Occupation Medal was intended only for members of the United States Army but was expanded in 1948 to encompass the United States Air Force shortly after that service's creation.

★ ★ ★ ★ ★

Korean Service Medal

The Korean Service Medal is a military award for service in the United States Armed Forces and was created in November 1950 by executive order of Pres. Harry Truman. The Korean Service Medal is the primary United States military award for participation in the Korean War and is awarded to any U.S. serviceman who performed duty within territorial limits or service that directly supported the UN's military efforts in defense of South Korea between 1950 and 1954.

★ ★ ★ ★ ★

Vietnam Service Medal

The Vietnam Service Medal is a military award of the United States Armed Forces established on July 8, 1965, by order of Pres. Lyndon B. Johnson.

★ ★ ★ ★ ★

JERRY L. BURTON

Formal Education after High School

University of Missouri,
    at Kansas City BA Economics 1955
Air Force Institute of Technology,
    Wright-Patterson AFB, Ohio, MBA

Nonmilitary Employment

I worked for a number of different companies and was successful in sales.

Nonmilitary Flight Activity

I joined the local Kirtland AFB Aero club and the New Mexico Civil Air Patrol Wing in 1981. As a pilot, I flew every aircraft assigned to the wing and, during my tenure with the CAP, participated in two national natural disasters, the California Northridge Earthquake and Hurricane Katrina that struck New Orleans and the Gulf Coast states.

CAP Flight Line at Kirtland AFB, NM
Some of us who flew the T-34s

In addition to taking part in a number of search and rescue missions, I also flew numerous missions on the Mexico–New Mexico border for customs, border patrol, and Drug Enforcement Agency (DEA). My National Civil Air Patrol (CAP) membership expired in August 2011, and I did not renew. I spent thirty years flying for the CAP.

★ ★ ★ ★ ★

From time to time, agencies such as border patrol, customs, DEA, and the air force have asked CAP to provide certain services. Those missions have always been challenging, satisfying, and fun. Many of the adults in CAP, particularly the pilots, are active or retired military.

Rabbit and Hound

One such request involved the CAP role-playing as "drug smuggling" aircraft. The code name for the exercise was "rabbit and hound." The "rabbit" would be the CAP aircraft. The "hound" would be one or two military aircraft trying to find the "rabbit" and obtain the tail number. The game for us went something like this.

Another pilot, Ernie Braunschweig, and I met at the CAP Operation Room at Kirtland AFB very early. We had been briefed the previous day concerning what the air force was expecting from us. It was pretty simple. We were to fly a predefined route into that would take us about one hundred miles into Mexico. Then we would proceed on a northerly course. Our reentry would be someplace along the southern border of Arizona. Once we were back in the United States, we could take any route we wanted to get back to Albuquerque. If we saw the interceptors, we were authorized to make evasive maneuvers to prevent them from reading our tail number. They were not authorized to shoot us down. Thank goodness!

We did not know what kind of aircraft might intercept us, but we did know that their objective would be to obtain our tail number (registration number). The interceptors were on standby at one of the air bases in Arizona or New Mexico. They would be receiving information on our flight from one of the airborne radar balloons along the southern border. The radar information was downloaded real time to a ground operation center and quickly found its way to the interceptor pilots. They then would launch and fly in our direction to make the intercept. Once the pilots received contacts on their radar scope, they would complete the intercept and attempt to get close enough to read our tail number. Then they would slip away unseen. At least the intent was for them not to be seen by us.

Bill and I made a flight plan and obtained our release from the operations project officer for that mission. We performed our preflight inspection, climbed into our aircraft, and started the engine. The aircraft we were flying that day was a Cessna-206, a six-passenger, single-engine civilian airplane. After our pre-taxi checklist was completed, we called ground control and received taxi instructions and clearance to taxi. After we reached the intersection we had been directed to, we stopped, ran through our takeoff checklist, and called the tower for permission to take off. We taxied onto the runway, scanned the instruments one last time, cleared downfield, and smoothly advanced the throttle to full power. The seat backs pushed forward on our backs. We gained rotation speed, and I pulled back gently on the yolk to bring the nose wheel up off the runway. I held that pitch position until the main gear lifted free of the runway. Airspeed began to rapidly build. When it was just below climb speed, I applied just enough backpressure on the yolk to stop the airspeed needle on the climb airspeed. I continued the climb until we reached our cruise altitude. I leveled out, retrimmed the pitch, and let the airspeed build until it reached our planned cruise speed. Then I reduced the throttle a little until both the airspeed and altitude remained constant. When we were clear of the airport control area, I turned to a heading that would take me to Las Cruces.

Ernie and I sat back, relaxed, and struck up a conversation.

We finally reached the Las Cruces area and went descended and landed at the Las Cruces airport. After refueling and stretching our legs a little, we performed another preflight and took off for Mexico. Ernie was flying this leg of the mission.

It was important to maintain the assigned headings on this part of the flight so we didn't violate any airspace while we were actually in Mexico. We flew about 100 or 120 miles into Mexico, reached our designated turn point, and Ernie turned to a heading of due north. As we approached the Mexico–U.S. border, we descended to a very low altitude. We began scanning the sky for interceptor aircraft.

We crossed the border into Arizona, and things became a little tense. From this point on, we could be intercepted. We didn't know what kind of aircraft would intercept us. It could be a fast-flying military prop aircraft, or it could be a helicopter, or a fast- moving interceptor, or some kind of a special operations aircraft. We didn't know.

As soon as we crossed into Arizona, Ernie changed heading. He headed straight toward truth or consequences. We hugged the ground all the way and kept scanning for the interceptors. They could come on us from any direction now.

Well, we made it to T or C without seeing any interceptors, so we decided either we gave them the slip, or they we able to intercept us from our blind spots. We landed, sighed a big sigh, and asked the base operator to refuel or aircraft for the flight back to Kirtland AFB in Albuquerque.

Once again, we climbed back to our aircraft and prepared for takeoff. The mission seemed to be over, and we would find out when we got back to ops how it actually went. It had already been a very long day, and we were looking forward to a nice, relaxed flight back. Once airborne and out of the airport area, Ernie would probably close his eyes and take a little nap. I know I was ready for one.

We taxied out to the active runway, did our engine check, and ran the takeoff checklist. Ernie and I both checked the traffic pattern for other traffic. There was no traffic in sight, so we pulled onto the runway, added power, and we were homeward bound. It was going to be nice to get back.

I set the nose to climb speed, trimmed the airplane, and relaxed for what would be about a seven-minute climb to cruise altitude. We had been airborne maybe thirty seconds, and Ernie yelled, "Airplanes! Airplanes!" He was looking behind us. I quickly looked back while holding my course. Sure enough, there were two Air Force F-16s bearing down on us and closing fast, one on each side of us.

My military instincts kicked in. We were only five hundred feet above the ground. I pulled back on the yolk to raise the nose and kill off airspeed. The two jets were moving much faster than we were and might fly past us. My airspeed fell rapidly, and I lowered the nose and rolled to the left. As the nose sank below the horizon, I saw a very deep arroyo to the north. I pushed the nose over to gain airspeed and leveled my wings to check for the interceptors. No joy! That means we didn't see them. I kept my nose down to keep pushing the airspeed up. I rolled slightly the right to take another look for the fighters. I pulled two more steep turns, one in each direction, to look for the jets. Still, no joy. The arroyo came up fast, and I kept the nose down and pulled a high-g steep left turn and went down below the terrain into the arroyo.

I leveled the wings momentarily. Ernie yelled, "There one is!" I couldn't believe it. Out on my right wing, just behind the trailing edge and slightly high, was this F-16 with everything hung out except the wash! Wow, he sure looked big for a little fighter. I didn't fly that tight in formation when I was on active duty! The other fighter was a little farther behind and above my left wing.

I slowed more, but somehow they stayed with me. I added power and did a few more quick turns. All of a sudden, Ernie yelled at the top of his lungs, "Cable! Cable! Cable!" Now I had a huge cable in my face and two fighters on my wings! I pulled the nose up sharply and added full power. The jets broke out away from us.

Somehow we escaped the arroyo. Everything seemed to stand still for a moment. Then a message came over the radio, "Knock it off, knock it off." That was the phrase used to terminate a training engagement.

We looked around us to make sure we were clear and then turned to our heading for Albuquerque. We climbed to our cruising altitude. The adrenaline was still pretty high.

Suddenly, the two F-16s slipped into position, one off each wing tip. We were up to cruise airspeed by then, but they were able to drop speed brakes and stay with us. I looked out at the one on the left. Ernie looked out at the one on the right. They did a wing rock and departed up, up, and away!

I felt young again!

★ ★ ★ ★ ★

Hurricane Katrina

According to *USA Today*, Hurricane Katrina was a category 3 hurricane when it made landfall at 6:10 a.m. on August 29, 2005. The peak winds were around 120 mph. The surge of water did more direct damage than the winds. The average elevation of the city of New Orleans is one foot below sea level. The only flood controls for the city was a system of levees around and through the city. By 9:00 a.m., the levees began to break. The city was flooded. The water is as high as twenty feet in the city. Many people were stranded on their roofs.

The effect Katrina had on New Orleans was unlike any other hurricane I can remember. Water and electricity don't mix. The water wasn't going anywhere soon. The levees were no help because they were breaking, and the source of water, the Gulf of Mexico, was unlimited. So most of the city stayed flooded for several weeks. Instead of helping people "in place," the need became evacuation to somewhere dry like Houston, Albuquerque, and many other cities hundreds of miles from New Orleans.

139

Many others had already drowned. The Army Corps of Engineers began trying to repair the levees and pump water out of the city and back out to sea. It wasn't working. Bodies were floating in the streets, and others were lying on higher ground, rotting in the sun.

The National Guard was called in to do search and rescue along with the coast guard. The coast guard had an air station just off shore from the city. Search and rescue efforts were hampered by people shooting rifles at the rescue helicopters. The water was so high in most of the city that only boats could access the houses. Hundreds of people had been trapped inside their homes, and their bodies were inside and could not be recovered for more weeks because of the high water.

There was a nationwide call for help. I had placed my name on the CAP two-hour call list, along with a few other members. On September 8, shortly after noon, I received a call from the New Mexico Wing operations officer, Lt. Col. Jerry Burton, asking me if I could go to Baton Rouge, Louisiana, to do search and rescue and relief work for Katrina. He told me that he needed three people to make an open-ended commitment. He and Ernie Braunschweig were two, and I made three. At 2:00 p.m., the airplane, a new GA-8, was loaded and rolling down the runway for departure from Albuquerque (Kirtland AFB), New Mexico.

GippsAero GA-8

The GA-8 was not designed for speed. It was designed for operations in the outback of Australia. Top cruise speed was about 115–120 knots. It took us eight and one-half hours flying time to get to Baton Rouge. The good news of that is that we flew halfway on September 8, overnighted in Fort Worth.

We all slept well and got up very early so we could get to Baton Rouge before noon. When we had completed all the preboarding preflight activities, we boarded the aircraft. We ran the prestart checklist; all went well. Then we went down to the start engine part. I don't remember who was reading the checklist, but when they read, "Engage Starter," silence. With any other airplane, that wouldn't have been a problem. It wasn't the science of the airplane that was going to be the problem; it was the red tape of the bureaucracy that was about to stop us. CAP had contracted mechanics to support this Australian airplane. They were located at the home airfield of each aircraft. So the mechanics that we would normally call were in New Mexico. The New Mexico Wing operations officer was part of our crew, so Ernie and I decided he should be the one who handled the problem. A call was made to New Mexico Wing headquarters. They called Texas Wing to see if they could help; after all, we were in their state now. That didn't work out like we had hoped.

So the ops officer called wing headquarters again to get permission to use a local mechanic. The Fixed Base Operator (FBO) where we had parked for the night called their mechanic. He was a nice young guy who came over to the aircraft, and we explained the problem to him. He was not, of course, trained on this equipment, but wing had said he could look, but not touch. Most starting systems aren't that complex anyway. Ernie, a former engineer with Sandia National Labs, "shepherded" the young man around the airplane looking at generators, belts, switches, circuit breakers, etc. We all agreed that the problem was the starter. The ops officer gave him permission to touch everything.

We had opened up the cowls on the engine compartment and also removed the cover on the console. The best Texas Wing could do was suggest that they "might" be able to get one of their approved mechanics to come over the next day.

If you've ever done combat- or search-and-rescue or evacuation-type missions that are high priority, you can understand our frustration. We really were excited about this mission, and we wanted to go. Yes, combat missions were the same as this for several reasons. With combat missions, each one usually gets you closer to going home. But the greater reason for most of us was that once you throw the mental switch and get into the mind-set of flying a mission, you really, really want to fly the mission! It's just what you do.

When the mechanic looked at the starter, he said, "Oh, this is a foreign starter. It's complex, and I could really mess it up if I tried to get into it."

The ops officer was getting pretty impatient and asked us, "Any ideas?" None of us said anything. Then the young mechanic said, "Well, I've got one." The ops guy said, "Okay, that's one more than I have right now. What is it?" The young mechanic said, "It's called the tap test." Ernie laughed loudly. "Why didn't I think of that?" We looked at Ernie and asked, "What's a 'tap' test?" Ernie replied, "This is going to work. Just watch."

Well, it worked, and the airplane really did start we didn't want to shut it down. So we prepared to board and start except for the ops officer. If the engine started, he was going to run into the FBO ops and call New Mexico Wing and let them know that we were back on line again. I don't remember who was flying, but when we got to the part of the checklist where we were to engage the starter, one of us yelled, "Clear! Okay!" As the pilot engaged the starter, the mechanic struck the starter casing with a large wrench. Vroom! The engine started! Everyone laughed with relief as the ops officer ran back inside the FBO. In less than two minutes, he returned and boarded the aircraft through the rear door. Before he got in, he stopped and handed $30 to the young mechanic, who had intended to help us for free. But it was worth $10 to each of us to be on our way.

We had filed IFR thinking it would get us out of the Dallas area quicker. We were so wrong. It took us four hours to fly from Fort Worth to Baton Rouge.

When we got to Baton Rouge, the mission ops officer, a member of the Louisiana Wing, told us to keep the engine running. He had an immediate mission for us. He sent a passenger out to the aircraft with his baggage, and we were told to fly him up to another small airfield about an hour north, drop him off, and return to Baton Rouge. We did.

By the time we landed and got the aircraft taken care off, including getting an approved mechanic to check the starter, we had missed not only lunch but also supper. We were escorted to the makeshift dining room and found the floor completely covered, wall-to-wall with CAP aircrews asleep on the floor.

We were starved. We ordered a pizza to be delivered. We checked on motels, but they were all filled with evacuees from New Orleans. That night and the next, we slept on cots in the uniform storage closet. We slept pretty well, but we were not alone; there were mice. Only one ran across my face the first night.

As retired USAF officers, two of us pilot types, we arose early, dressed, and ready to go at about six. This time we missed breakfast. The dining room was still full of cots with sleeping CAP pilots.

JERRY L. BURTON

Breakfast wouldn't be available until about 7:30 a.m. But since we were up and ready, they assigned us a mission. We flew about a three-hour mission looking for breaks in the levees and reporting them to the Army Corps of Engineers.

We flew numerous missions per day. Some were search and rescue, and some were diplomatic flights of state and federal officials, including member of Congress and heads of various agencies.

One of the flights took us out over the Mississippi River Delta. Most of the delta was under five to ten feet of water. There were numerous boats adrift or grounded. We were looking for floating bodies. You could clearly see the navigation channels beneath the floodwater. We had heard that the dolphins from the Audubon Aquarium of the Americas in New Orleans had escaped. We saw them swimming up one of the flooded canals, jumping through the air, submerging, jumping. It was a refreshingly beautiful sight amid all the death and debris, such as caskets in trees.

The members of the National Congress of American Indians were our passengers on one flight. We covered a lot of ground that day. Every representative wanted to see their parishes to assess the damage so they could estimate the amount of relief money to request. I was surprised at the number of "parishes" that are Indian. They were the most fun bunch of people we had as passengers. They interacted a lot.

One of the missions we refused would have required us to transport fifty gallon drums of hazardous materials that had surfaced on the shores of Lake Pontchartrain near the Louis Armstrong International Airport. We were asked to help load them into our aircraft with only plastic gloves as protective gear. I don't remember what the chemicals were, but they were very dangerous, and the operation officer called New Mexico Wing and told them he would not allow the wing aircraft to be used on that mission. The New Mexico Wing commander concurred. I think the plan was changed, and the drums were transported by military land vehicles.

One of the major goals of CAP in getting involved in the Katrina operation was to "showcase" the GA-8 to obtain funding for more of the aircraft. Personally, I thought the GA-8 to be an excellent aircraft for the multiple missions of CAP. Unfortunately, I think the CPA command structure was too anxious to showcase the aircraft while compromising the aircrew. Another example of this was that there had been a waiver granted on reducing the crew rest requirement. At least that is what was conveyed to us.

After six continuous days of long flights, which in itself was fine, we taxied in as the sun was approaching the horizon in the west. We were really looking forward to sitting, eating a nice meal—the food was good when we happened to be scheduled to eat—and then hitting the sack early. Before we could get to the food line, we were told that we needed to get the aircraft refueled, load all our personal equipment into the airplane, and immediately depart for Tyndall AFB in Florida. Florida needed us over there, and since all three of us were retired air force lieutenant colonels, we were the most logical to go. We asked the Louisiana ops guy to have three sandwiches and drinks ready for us when we departed. He did.

So tired, hungry, and pretty stinky, we filed an IFR flight plan and too off for Tyndall near Panama City, Florida, as the sun was sinking behind us. Our New Mexico Wing operations officer, Jerry, had gone through intercept training at Tyndall years ago. Half the base had been damaged significantly, but he assured us it would be better than what we had experienced at Baton Rouge. Of course, in defense of Baton Rouge, they did a very fine and professional job considering what they had to work with. Their city had become the landing zone for thousands of refugees from New Orleans. So a tip of the hat to them!

We had been pushed to get airborne because the air operations at Tyndall shut down each night at 2200 or 10:00 p.m. When we were roughly thirty miles out, we contacted the tower at Tyndall. They told us that they were closing in less than ten minutes and to go away. We told them that we had been directed to come to Tyndall at the request of the base, and they had been notified of our coming and had also been told that they would remain open until we arrived. There was silence. Then they responded that they had one person who had volunteered to stay until we were down.

We kept our speed up and put the wheels on the runway down field close to the taxiway by the tower. We arrived at about five or six minutes after 10:00 p.m. We taxied to the base passenger terminal and met the two men from Florida CAP who would be coordinating our missions while we were there. They were outstanding. They had warm coffee for us, personally provided transportation to the BOQ for us, and they had already checked us in and had individual rooms and keys for us.

Our mission while at Tyndall was to transport damage assessment teams to the various military facilities on the Gulf Coast. Most flights would take us from Tyndall to Coast Guard Air Station New Orleans. We would drop the DA team there for morning meetings. After the meetings, we would go to the assigned location(s) for the day. The CG Air Station did not have our level of aviation fuel, so if the DA team were not going over to Louis Armstrong International, where there was a military installation that had been damaged, we would fly the GA–8 over to Louis Armstrong during the morning meeting and refuel it there at the civilian FBO, which did have our grade of fuel.

140

This is the Lake Pontchartrain Causeway. We flew over it on final approach into Louis Armstrong. The airport was legally closed the entire time we were there. The runways were partially flooded, and there was damage to many of the buildings. There was enough "dry" runway for us to land and a dry taxiway also. We didn't require much distance to land. We were exempted from the closure because we were a disaster relief operation.

The DA teams would generally work until 6:00 p.m. (1800). That would allow them to get supper before we returned to Tyndall. We had sack lunches. We always got back to base around 10:00 or 10:15 p.m. (2200 or 2215). It became standard procedure for one controller to volunteer to stay until we were back in the nest.

So our standard day began with the Florida CAP ops guys. One in particular took great care of us, and we jokingly called him Mom. They would get to ops about 0430 (4:30 a.m.), file our standard flight plan with our standard routing, make sure the aircraft was fully fueled unless we had told them otherwise, have all the paperwork, passenger manifest, and release forms ready so that all we had to do was sign them. They would have everything printed out and laid out on the counter so we could just walk move from one stack to another and sign them.

The one we called Mom would already knew what we liked for breakfast, so he would go by the mess hall before he went to ops and order our breakfast and ask that it be ready to eat at 0500. At 0455, he would be at the curb outside the BOQ, and so would we. He'd take us straight to the mess hall so we would get started with a great breakfast. The other "Mom" would make sure the aircraft was ready and the DA team was on time; 0545 was their showtime.

We'd finish breakfast by 0530 and then go straight to flight ops. Our paperwork and ground preflight would be completed by the time the DA team showed. We'd walk into flight ops and introduce ourselves, do a roll call, tell them to go to the restrooms, get their stuff, and meet us at the aircraft. We'd always give them the tail number so they would go to the correct aircraft. Once they loaded, we called roll one more time. One of the "Moms" would come out to the aircraft and get a signed copy of the passenger manifest for the file. We were on our takeoff roll by 0600 or 0605 every morning. 0600 was the first allowed departure time.

Our route took us south of the coastline, about twenty-five miles out over the Gulf. We were over water until we landed at CG New Orleans. The return route was usually a little different. We always flew out over the Gulf unless we were on approach to Biloxi or one of the other military bases on the coast.

Crew rest was in a chair in the terminal building or on the tarmac in the shadow of the wing of the aircraft. I would roll up one of the blankets from the aircraft and use it as a pillow.

We made multiple flights a day for ten days straight and logged over four hours a day. We didn't always fly together as a crew. Often, we would carry nine passengers—one would sit in the copilot position.

We ended the deployment on a flight to Clinton, Alabama, where we left the aircraft for another crew to use. The flight from Tyndall was almost totally in heavy rain and fog. We were driven to Maxwell AFB, checked into the BOQ there, and then taken by ground transportation personnel the next morning to the civilian airport in Montgomery. It took forever to get our baggage checked in because we had one-way tickets, and because 9/11 was still on everyone's mind, we checked everything but our teeth.

We were really tired. It was nice to fly and be able to close your eyes. But we were proud to have sacrificed and served. That's what we do!

★ ★ ★ ★ ★

Once a month, a bunch of us "old-timers" from CAP get together for breakfast. I'm the good-looking fellow with glasses, wearing a black jacket, next to the man wearing a blue jacket.

FAMILY

Mary Lou and I eventually moved into a retirement home. Our children were all grown and gone.

We lost one girl, Deborah, the eldest. She was up in Alaska. She got a cancer on the base of her brain. She was about thirty-seven years old when she passed away.

My second eldest girl, Miriam, was also in Alaska. She was there with her husband. Then her husband died about eight months later with an aneurism on the brain. He had been building houses for the Eskimos up there.

So I only have five of my children still here. Miriam, who is a retired nurse from UNM Hospital, is the only one here in Albuquerque. Martha lives in Salt Lake City. Her husband was a graduate of the Air Force Academy.

And sadly, I lost Mary Lou in 2014.

Mary Lou (Maloney) Drumm

February 13, 2014

A wonderful wife, mother, and grandmother to her family, she was a gifted source to coworkers, a brilliant mathematician to her teachers, a cum laude graduate, and a delightful companion to her friends.

A dry sense of humor, laughter, and love filled her lifetime.

Mary Lou is survived by her husband, William H. Drumm, and five of her children—David Drumm, Michael Drumm, Daniel Drumm, Miriam Plett, and Martha Chapman. Mary Lou was preceded in death by her daughter, Deborah Bove.

Family Military Heritage

As already mentioned, Martha's husband graduated from the United States Air Force Academy. He flew F–86s with the wing that was stationed in Salt Lake City. He had about twelve years with the air force and resigned his commission to go with Delta Airlines. He's a senior captain with Delta now.

They have a son who's a medivac helicopter pilot. He was in Afghanistan and had about fifteen or twenty missions. He was a platoon leader. He graduated from the University of Westminster but took his ROTC at Utah. He moved right along through Fort Rucker in his helicopter training and then went to Fort Campbell.

My nephew's son got out of high school and went into the marines and was over in Iraq and Afghanistan for four years. He came back, got out of the marines for one year, and then joined the navy as a SEAL.

He's been a SEAL for three or four years now. He received a Bronze Star; we don't know what it's for, of course. Just recently, I heard that he's in the hospital. He did something and broke his hip. When he was in training with the SEALs, he broke a leg.

When he graduated into the SEALs, we asked him if he had a specialty. He said, "Yes, I'm going to be a driver." I said, "You mean you did all this training just to drive a vehicle?" He said, "No, Grandpa. I'm going to drive a submarine." So I asked, "What kind of submarine are you talking about?"

He told me that the navy now has a number of smaller submarines. So he's an official submarine driver now.

My brother was a pilot during World War II. He was not overseas until after the war. He was in class 45A, so the war was already over before he got out. Bob also had twenty-eight years of service when he retired.

He had two sons. One is a West Point Graduate. Both of his boys are retired now.

Bob's son, Michael, was in Iraq, Bosnia, and Kosovo. He flew Mohawks.

His other son, Bobby, the one out of West Point, got up to be an O-6. He worked for a while in Rumsfeld's office. He later retired. He got himself a job as a GS-15 in the office he was working in when he retired from the military. Subsequently, he has moved to the Homeland Security Office, where he's gone past the GS-16 and into some other designation and is doing really well in that.

My wife's father was in World War I.

I had an aunt, Sadie, who was also in World War I. She was the army nurse over in France.

Then of course, there's "Dolly," my navy cousin. She's the one I saw on my way back from CBI. She was a WAVE.

PRIDE IN OUR HERITAGE

We've had at least one family member in every war since World War I. And we have two of them on active duty now, the SEAL and the one who just returned from Afghanistan.

Members of the military are part of one large family. It's a proud family, and it's a loving family. Friendships made during military service are seldom broken. The passage of time dims all memory, but military experiences and friendships don't dim quickly.

In October 2003, Susan Ronnenkamp Boatright, daughter of Bill Drumm's engineer, George G. Ronnenkamp, found the museum webpage and the crew photo taken at Gowen Field.

She contacted Gayle, at Gowen Field, and asked if it were possible to contact Mr. Drumm the pilot. Her father was also very pleased to learn "that anyone had an interest in what we did there." Most of us don't expect to ever be part of a display in a museum.

Gayle contacted me, and I told her that I had been trying to locate George and the rest of the crew for the past thirty years. This was the best news I had received about the crew since we split in Karachi.

George had actually been looking for me years as well. Every time I went TDY, temporary duty, the first thing I would do was grab a phone book and look for his name.

After Gayle put us in contact with each other, the years just melted away. Over that Thanksgiving holiday, our families were reunited.

What a blessing!

★ ★ ★ ★ ★

"COLLAGE of Bill's Family is on the last page of this book"

CHAPTER 21

The Enemy Within: Clouds of the Future Wars

I, WILLIAM HENRY Drumm, Jr., do solemnly swear that I will support and defend the Constitution of the United States against all enemies, foreign and domestic; that I will bear true faith and allegiance to the same; and that I will obey the orders of the President of the United States and the orders of the officers appointed over me, according to regulations and the Uniform Code of Military Justice. So help me God.[141]

On the first of December 1942, I was sworn into the Army Reserve Corps as part of the U.S. Army Air Forces Aviation Cadet Program.

When I first took that oath, the threat to this country was foreign. It was remote. It was a "world away." It was Germany, the nation of Nazis who were invading and conquering other nations on the European continent. It was Japan, the rising imperialist nation in the Far East, who had virtually destroyed much of our navy at Pearl Harbor.

As an officer in the United States Air Force, there was another code to which I had to commit. That was the U.S. Military Code of Conduct.

1. *I am an American fighting in the forces that guard my country and our way of life. I am prepared to give my life in their defense.*
2. *I will never surrender of my own free will. If in command, I will never surrender the members of my command while they still have the means to resist.*
3. *If I am captured, I will continue to resist by all means available. I will make every effort to escape and aid others to escape. I will accept neither parole nor special favors from the enemy.*
4. *If I become a prisoner of war, I will keep faith with my fellow prisoners. I will give no information nor take part in any action which might be harmful to my comrades.*
5. *If I am senior, I will take command. If not, I will obey the lawful orders of those appointed over me and will back them up in every way.*
6. *Should I become a prisoner of war, I am required to give name, rank, service number, and date of birth. I will evade answering further questions to the utmost of my ability. I will make no oral or written statements disloyal to my country and its allies.*
7. *I will never forget that I am an American fighting for freedom, responsible for my actions, and dedicated to the principles which made my country free. I will trust in my God and in the United States of America.*

At ninety-six years old, I remain resolute in my oaths. But now in the year 2020, the enemy is domestic. It is here, in our country, and they are determined to destroy "our country and our way of life." They want to take away the freedoms I fought for and remove "the principles that made my country free."

How did they get here? We have invited them in. There's an old saying: "Nice guys never win." As a freedom-loving, compassionate nation, we extend ourselves to help others. This nation gives almost twice as much foreign aid as any other free-world country. We also strive to lift those in lower socioeconomic situations.

This nation proudly allows free speech. The assumption is that every voice deserves to be heard and taken seriously. What the Communists and socialists have figured out is that they can say anything they want without consequences. Freedom of the press allows the media to do the same thing.

So we as a country are easy to criticize for three major reasons. First, our Constitution allows it because the Constitution values individuals; second, there are no consequences to critical speech about someone unless the speaker is encouraging violence or threatening to seriously harm another person; and third, as a nation, we, the people, are sincerely interested in every voice being heard—respectfully and without fear of reprisal.

After World War 1, France wanted to devastate Germany. They did a pretty good job of that for a while. Great Britain, like France, had been devastated by Germany. But Great Britain realized that they should look to the greater good of rebuilding their nation and normalizing trade in Europe. Devastating Germany was not a good idea. The United States advocated for the rebuilding of Germany for the good people who lived there and for the sake of future generations in all nations by establishing normal and good relationships, particularly in commerce, among all nations. The United States even paid much of Germany's war reparations from World War I. That generosity played a large role in the coming of the Great Depression.

Most people who study history would agree that World War II involved four countries that were attempting to emerge as world empires. They were Germany, Japan, Italy, and the Soviet Union. There were two countries that were declining as empires and were hoping to survive. Those two countries were Great Britain and France. The United States didn't care about being an empire, but they certainly wanted to raise their standard of living for everyone through strong international commerce. So they allied with Great Britain because of the commercial investments they had made prior to the war.

JERRY L. BURTON

After World War II, it was the United States that "engineered" the recovery plans for Europe and Japan. The United States actually financed their recoveries, again, by investing in them. Both sides of the investment process won.

So how does the United States get a bad rap on this? To answer this questions, I think we have to consider the alternatives to what we are. The United States is, I believe, best characterized as a Constitutional Federal Republic with a representative form of democracy. That is, we are a republic of fifty states with Federal oversight (elected by representatives of the states). The representatives were elected by majority vote of the individual constituents of the state (democracy).

Finally, democracies and republics stem from a very different view of human nature. Democracies believe the people are inherently well intended. To the degree that this is true, the best decisions will receive the greater popular support. Republics, on the other hand, have an inherent distrust of human nature. That is why they have a set of laws in place and require obedience to those laws. This is a way of maintaining an expected level of peace and order. I think this is one of the strongest characteristics of our system. On the one hand, it expects most of the people to be good. On the other hand, it declares a certain level of good behavior and a path to dealing with those who fail to behave as the majority would require. Finally, most of these guidelines (laws), though they may have been set at the federal or state level, can be changed by the people themselves by a majority vote. A few issues, like Amendments to the U.S. Constitution, require a lot more effort by the design of the founders of the Constitution.

I think about the other forms of governing that are in the minds of insurgents and wonder why they think their form of government is better than ours. Marxism (Communism), socialism, aristocracy, progressivism (politically enlightened), liberalism, conservatism, nationalism, dictatorship, global governance, and social democracy are some of the terms I've heard over the years.

Many of these are not threats to the United States. For example, liberalism, conservatism, and nationalism are terms that are thrown around a lot these days, but they are not forms of government; they are attitudes that affect the manner in which one governs. The meanings of these terms have been modified so much lately by the politicians and the news media that I think they've lost their effectiveness.

Liberalism is most often defined as an attitude of nonjudgment for that which is different. That is, a liberal is open to new, different, and even contradictory ideas without judging them as good or bad. Liberals are accepting of things and thoughts different from what their norms are. They are not prejudice or biased to any degree on anything. Frankly, that sounds more like the conservatives I know than the liberals.

Conservatives are most often defined as people who are unwilling to accept any new ideas or changes in habit, culture, or custom. Their own ideas are the only valid ones—no discussion allowed. Sounds like most of the liberals I know. But in all fairness, I do believe very deeply in one facet of conservatism: "If it ain't broke, don't fix it!" Actually, I thin conservatives are quicker to actually fix or improve things than liberals.

The threats to our way of life is from people who see problems in our existing system of government, and their solution is to abandon our way of governing, still the best system in the world even with its many flaws, and trash it for something totally different and less desirable.

Nationalism is another term that has been used as a scare tactic by the left. Nationalism is a love for one's national language and customs. It spans generations of offspring and years of investment of self and is usually a source of great personal pride. I am nationalistic when I say that I am proud to be an American. I am even proud of the achievements of the American people. And I truly believe that we are unique and among the greatest people on earth. A lot of this feeling comes from the fact that America is a meritocracy. That is, people advance in society and business on the basis of merit. You are who you are, what you are, and where you are based largely on what you have been able to achieve or do. The idea of meritocracy came under attack years ago when little league stopped giving "winners" trophies and everyone got a "participation" trophy. Competition builds excellence. If I want a nice meal, I'm more likely to go to Ruth's Chris than to a burger joint. If I'm in an air battle, I definitely want the winner's trophy! If I'm working harder and longer than the person beside me, then I have rightly earned more than that person. If that person suffers some kind of a disability that disallows him or her to work as hard and long as I, then reason and compassion require some consideration for the welfare of that person. Where our form of government might not do that, our charitable institutions should.

Dictatorships are pretty easy to explain. That's what you get after you overthrow an existing government and bring about the chaos that Karl Marx thought would naturally resolve itself to communism. Marx, of course, attacked capitalism because it is competitive, and he didn't compete well.

Marxism and most forms of socialism hold the position that mankind, given the opportunity to make their own choices and the freedom to do whatever they want and not have to worry about money, food, or competition, will rise to the highest level of development and satisfaction possible for them. Each person becomes "perfect" in his or herself, and all the relationships among all other people become perfect because there is no competition. It's interesting to me that the Marxists and socialists think that perfection comes from lack of competition. I don't recall seeing any level of perfection in the hippy communes. In addition to the free love and drugs, there were thefts, murders, lying, and exploitation of women and weaker men. Money was also a high priority in the communes. In certain areas near the Navajo, Pueblo, and Hopi markets, it was customary to throw your blanket on the plaza and lay out your wares. This scene was so loved by tourists, but that scene was soon changed. The hippies took over about 60–70 percent of the plaza area that had been the market place for Indians.

A dictatorship has resulted from every occasion I know of where a country had turned to communism. In the case of Russia, China, Cuba, and to the best of my limited knowledge, every South and

Central American and Middle Eastern dictatorship, the change of power has included the execution of hundreds to millions of political opponents.

An aristocracy is a government run by a few people who are considered to be well-qualified to govern by virtue of their education, experience, or connections. The French, British, and Canadian governments might generally be ruled by such people. Outsiders are known as commoners.

The three remaining forms of government, social democratic, progressive, and global governance are the concerning ones. The social democrats advocate a gradual and peaceful transition from capitalism to socialism. They propose that this would be done by democratic means. The new state would be a welfare state incorporating capitalist and socialist practices.

Social democracy and progressivism are almost identical. Both would come about by taking over the Congress and passing legislation that makes the transition. All production activities would then be owned and directed by the government. The owners of businesses would become managers and workers in those business, or they would be placed somewhere else in the work force. That would be entirely up to the government. There would be no meritorious considerations—everyone would get a wage that was set by the government. There would only be one public standard of living. The "duly" elected representatives of Congress (that's the democratic part of this government) would get whatever they "democratically" decided.

That's not too different from the way Congress operates now. The Affordable Care Act, "Obama Care," is a great example of how social democracy would work. Congress does something that is supposed to help the "commoner." And it might help them. But if I remember correctly, Congress had its own health-care plans. Theirs was head and shoulders above "Obama Care," and it was free—to Congress!

Progressives are simply socialists who don't want the stigma of the name socialist. There is another difference that is rapidly disappearing. The progressives tout their compassion for the less fortunate. Therefore, they have a "moral" selling point. The socialists are certainly picking up on that. The younger generations are seeing the progressives and the socialists as having the higher moral ground.

Raising the income of the less fortunate should always be in our sights. However, I suspect income equality will be reached by adjusting the incomes of the people to bare subsistence while raising the income of the government as a reward for leveling peasant income. That's the way it seems to have worked in other countries.

There is a term used among the progressives, "enlightened." From the mouth of two local progressive activists in Albuquerque, one a retired college professor and one an activist website host, if you are one of the "enlightened" ones, then you will see and support the progression from democracy to socialism. That also means that you will be among the "ruling" class.

The last style of governing is one that almost slipped by four years ago. That is what I call one-world government. It's a bit like having the United Nations take over as the global government. However, the controllers of the government would be a collection of the wealthiest people and most influential people on earth. The rich would get richer, and the poor would get poorer. And the entire middle class would disappear. I think this was the direction and goal of the country after the election twelve years ago.

That's what I think would happen with social democracy and progressivism as well.

All these plans discussed above and the fact that there are powers attempting to ruin our Constitutional Federal Republic are actually tracking along a progressive plan to overthrow our government. That insurgency plan was read into the *Congressional Record* back in 1963 by Democratic Congressman Albert S. Herlong Jr. of Florida. The list was derived from a book, *The Naked Communist*, by researcher Cleon Skousens:[142]

1. U.S. should accept coexistence as the only alternative to atomic war.
2. U.S. should be willing to capitulate in preference to engaging in atomic war. [Note: These encapsulate the Kennan Doctrine, which advocated for the "containment" of communism. Establishment figures supporting the amoral containment policy at least implicitly worked with the communists in scaring the wits out of the American people concerning atomic war. President Ronald Reagan undid the doctrine when he took an aggressive stand against the Evil Empire by backing freedom fighters from around the world that were struggling against the left-wing communist jackboot. As a result, the Soviet Union and its satellites imploded, a considerable and unexpected setback to the international communist edifice.]
3. Develop the illusion that total disarmament by the U.S. would be a demonstration of "moral strength." [Note: The nuclear freeze advocates supported a freeze on American nuclear development only. Rarely were Soviet nukes or those of other nations mentioned in their self-righteous tirades. The same advocates now call for reducing American military might, claiming that there is something immoral about America preserving its military pre-eminence in the world.]
4. Permit free trade between all nations regardless of Communist affiliation and regardless of whether or not items could be used for war. [Note: Today, there are calls to end the embargo on the slave island of Cuba, there were complaints about the embargo against Iraq, and the U.S., not Saddam Hussein, was blamed for the suffering of the Iraqi people. Would they have advocated for free trade with Hitler and his National Socialist regime?]
5. Extend long-term loans to Russia and Soviet satellites.
6. Provide American aid to all nations regardless of Communist domination. [Note: Such aid and trade over decades contributed greatly to the left-wing communist liquidation

of over 100 million people worldwide, according to the well-documented "Black Book of Communism." This aid and trade marks a shameful chapter in American history. Without the aid and trade, the left-wing international communist behemoth would have imploded on its own rot a lot sooner and umpteen millions would have been saved from poverty, misery, starvation and death.]

7. Grant recognition of Red China and admission of Red China to the U.N. [Note: Not only did President Jimmy Carter fulfill this goal but he also betrayed America's allies in Nicaragua, El Salvador, Iran, Afghanistan, Angola and elsewhere.]

8. Set up East and West Germany as separate states in spite of Khrushchev's promise in 1955 to settle the Germany question by free elections under supervision of the U.N.

9. Prolong the conferences to ban atomic tests because the U.S. has agreed to suspend tests as long as negotiations are in progress.

10. Allow all Soviet satellites individual representation in the U.N.

11. Promote the U.N. as the only hope for mankind. If its charter is rewritten, demand that it be set up as a one-world government with its own independent armed forces. [Note: There are still American intellectuals, and elected members of Congress, who dream of an eventual one world government and who view the U.N., founded by communists such as Alger Hiss, the first secretary-general, as the instrument to bring this about. World government was also the dream of Adolf Hitler and J.V. Stalin. World government was the dream of Osama bin Laden and the 9/11 hijackers.]

12. Resist any attempt to outlaw the Communist Party. [Note: While the idea of banning any political party runs contrary to notions of American freedom and liberty, notions that are the exact opposite of those held by the left-wing communists themselves, nevertheless these goals sought to undermine the constitutional obligation of Congress to investigate

subversion. The weakening of our government's ability to conduct such investigations led to the attack of 9/11.]

13. Do away with loyalty oaths. [Note: It is entirely proper and appropriate for our government to expect employees, paid by the American taxpayer, to take an oath of loyalty.]

14. Continue giving Russia access to the U.S. Patent Office.

15. Capture one or both of the political parties in the U.S. [Note: In his book, "Reagan's War," Peter Schweizer demonstrates the astonishing degree to which communists and communist sympathizers have penetrated the Democratic Party. In his book, Schweizer writes about the presidential election of 1979.]

16. Use technical decisions of the courts to weaken basic American institutions, by claiming their activities violate civil rights. [Note: This strategy goes back to the founding of the American Civil Liberties Union by Fabian Socialists Roger Baldwin and John Dewey and Communists William Z. Foster and Elizabeth Gurley Flynn among others.]

17. Get control of the schools. Use them as transmission belts for Socialism and current Communist propaganda. Soften the curriculum. Get control of teachers associations. Put the party line in textbooks.

18. Gain control of all student newspapers.

19. Use student riots to foment public protests against programs or organizations that are under Communist attack. [Note: The success of these goals, from a communist perspective, is obvious. Is there any doubt this is so?]

20. Infiltrate the press. Get control of book review assignments, editorial writing, policy-making positions.

21. Gain control of key positions in radio, TV & motion pictures.

22. Continue discrediting American culture by degrading all form of artistic expression. An American Communist cell was told to "eliminate all good sculpture from parks and buildings," substituting shapeless, awkward and meaningless forms.

23. Control art critics and directors of art museums. "Our plan is to promote ugliness, repulsive, meaningless art."
24. Eliminate all laws governing obscenity by calling them "censorship" and a violation of free speech and free press.
25. Break down cultural standards of morality by promoting pornography and obscenity in books, magazines, motion pictures, radio and TV. [Note: This is the Gramscian agenda of the "long march through the institutions" spelled out explicitly: gradual takeover of the "means of communication" and then using those vehicles to debauch the culture and weaken the will of the individual to resist.]
26. Present homosexuality, degeneracy and promiscuity as "normal, natural and healthy." [Note: Today those few who still have the courage to advocate public morality are denounced and viciously attacked. Most Americans are entirely unwitting regarding the motives behind this agenda.]
27. Infiltrate the churches and replace revealed religion with "social" religion. Discredit the Bible and emphasize the need for intellectual maturity, which does not need a "religious crutch." [Note: This has been largely accomplished through the communist infiltration of the National Council of Churches, Conservative and Reform Judaism, and the Catholic seminaries.]
28. Eliminate prayer or any phase of religious expression in the schools on the grounds that it violates the principle of "separation of church and state"
29. Discredit the American Constitution by calling it inadequate, old fashioned, out of step with modern needs, a hindrance to cooperation between nations on a worldwide basis.
30. Discredit the American founding fathers. Present them as selfish aristocrats who had no concern for the "common man."
31. Belittle all forms of American culture and discourage the teaching of American history on the ground that it was only a minor part of "the big picture." Give more emphasis to Russian history since the Communists took over. [Note:

Obliterating the American past, with its antecedents in principles of freedom, liberty and private ownership is a major goal of the communists then and now.]

32. Support any socialist movement to give centralized control over any part of the culture – education, social agencies, welfare programs, mental health clinics, etc.

33. Eliminate all laws or procedures which interfere with the operation of the Communist apparatus.

34. Eliminate the House Committee on Un-American Activities.

35. Discredit and eventually dismantle the FBI.

36. Infiltrate and gain control of more unions.

37. Infiltrate and gain control of big business.

38. Transfer some of the powers of arrest from the police to social agencies. Treat all behavioral problems as psychiatric disorders which no one but psychiatrists can understand or treat. [Note: The Soviets used to send "social misfits" and those deemed politically incorrect to massive mental institutions called gulags. The Red Chinese call them lao gai. Hitler called them concentration camps.]

39. Dominate the psychiatric profession and use mental health laws as a means of gaining coercive control over those who oppose communist goals. [Note: Psychiatry remains a bulwark of the communist agenda of fostering self-criticism and docility.]

40. Discredit the family as an institution. Encourage promiscuity and easy divorce. [Note: Done! The sovereign family is the single most powerful obstacle to authoritarian control.]

41. Emphasize the need to raise children away from the negative influence of parents. Attribute prejudices, mental blocks and retarding of children to suppressive influence of parents. [Note: Outcome-based education, values clarification or whatever they're calling it this year.]

42. Create the impression that violence and insurrection are legitimate aspects of the American tradition; that students and special interest groups should rise up and make a "united

force" to solve economic, political or social problems. [Note: This describes the dialectical fostering of group consciousness and conflict, which furthers the interests of authoritarianism.]

43. Overthrow all colonial governments before native populations are ready for self-government.
44. Internationalize the Panama Canal.
45. Repeal the Connally Reservation so the U.S. cannot prevent the World Court from seizing jurisdiction over domestic problems. Give the World Court jurisdiction over domestic problems. Give the World Court jurisdiction over nations and individuals alike.

What We Can Do within the System

In December 1941, I said, "It was time for my generation to step up!" Now almost fifty-nine years later, I'm saying, "It's time for real Americans to step up!"

Voting Problems

As an individual citizen, I only have one vote and one voice. In a country with a population of roughly 331 million,[143] it seems that my vote hardly counts. So how could I possibly make a difference?

I can't begin to answer the question until I've surveyed the battlefield. The deciding battle is at the ballot box. So I would look at the "election battlefield" first.

The *Federal Register*,[144] a U.S. government publication, estimates the number of people in the United States of voting age to be about 253.8 million. The "turnout" rate, those people who actually bothered to cast their vote, in the 2018 midterm was about 50.3 percent.[145] In the previous presidential election, in 2016, the turnout was 60 percent.[146]

The highest turnout rate in a national election since 2002 was 62.2 percent in 2008.[147] That means about 96 million people didn't vote in that election. The average turnout since 1908 has fluctuated between 50 and 60 percent.[148]

New Mexico, where I now live, has an estimated population of 2.1 million people, 1.5 million[149] of whom are eligible to vote. Voter turnout in the 2018 midterm election was only 47 percent.[150] Voter turnout in the previous presidential election of 2016 was a little better at 55 percent.[151]

2016 67,000 vote difference   House Vote
2018 3,000 vote difference   House Vote
2018 164,000 vote difference   Senate Vote

NM Registration by Party[152]:

	Dem	Rep	Lib	Indep	Other
Total:	579,409	384,937	11,189	285,111	12,949 Total: 1,273,595
	45.5%	30.2%	0.9%	22.4%	1%

Turnout:
2016 385,234   319,667   74,541 18,877   Defected: 264,420
     68.4%   85.3% 905.6%   6.7% 283,297   93.3%   66,310 Indep + Other defectors just to Lib Party

     2018 376,998 212,813 107,201   Defected: 98,970
          66.9% 56.8% 130.2%   283,297 34.9%

Turnout for school board elections usually run well below a dismal 10 percent![153]

So on the national level, there are roughly 101 million eligible voters who do not vote in our elections. In my state of New Mexico, less than 55 percent[154] of eligible voters typically show up for any election. The no-shows amount to roughly 650,000 voters.

JERRY L. BURTON

Voting is a critical right and responsibility that we have as citizens of this country. In a true democracy, the majority rules. In the United States, we are lucky if a majority of the eligible voters even show up!

Who are these nonvoters, why are they not voting, and how do we get them to the polls so their voices can be heard and they can be fairly represented?

Voter information is public, and the Secretary of State for each state has the identification of each registered voter, where they live and when they did and did not vote. State and local political parties could, if they were run properly, obtain this information and contact the voter (if they really exist) and determine why they are not voting and offer them assistance in becoming an active voice at the polls. To a degree, this is already being done. It's called the voter purge process. It happens after every major (presidential) election.

The head of each registered party in a state is given a list of the registered voters as of the last election. The list show the names and addresses and voting record of each person listed. A representative of each party goes through the list and tries to determine if each person on the register is still alive and still a resident of the state. Typically, each party checks the voters of the other party(ies). This is just one step in the attempt to prevent voter fraud.

Recommendation: An outside, nonpolitical group should audit the purge of names and recheck it before the next election to make sure previously deleted names have not been reentered.

Recommendation: VOTER PICTURE ID at the polls should be required by every state. If it is not in your state, you need to work to get it.

INSURGENCY PROBLEMS

Insurgency is an effort to overthrow an existing government. It is made to look like an internal struggle but is usually influenced or even instigated by an outside power. The tactics involve deception, disinformation, demonstrations, and riots over "injustices" and propagandizing. An insurgency operation is designed to overthrow a sitting government from within. A government such as ours, because of our belief in freedom of speech and a free press, can be overthrown by using lies, deception, and illogical arguments and ridiculous accusations that uninformed or poorly educated people will believe.

Insurgency, because there are no armies killing people, can take a very long time to succeed. That's because the insurgents are actually changing the way the people think and believe. The most effective means of controlling the way people think and believe is to discredit the truth and replace it with a lie. The most effective ways of achieving this are to:

1. control what is taught in the schools—this was called brainwashing when I was young;
2. control the media—radio, newspapers, magazines, internet content—in other words, spread propaganda to achieve the desired ends; and
3. influence the electoral process by

   a. allowing people who are not eligible to vote to do so,
   b. allowing people to vote twice,
   c. allowing people to vote under someone else's name,
   d. intimidating people into voting a certain way,
   e. illegally modifying the electronic voting machines to produce certain results, and
   f. purposefully performing miscounts of ballets.

The following are all relatively easy to do, depending on what state you live in:

1. Pay rioters and demonstrators.
2. Bribe members of Congress.
3. Build distrust among the civilians and the police and military.

4. Always claim to be "protecting" the very people you are taking advantage of, and the list goes on.

Now I want to comment on some of the items in the insurgency plan of the Communist Party that was read into Congress in 1954. It will give us a "heads-up" for other things that are being done to destroy our way of life. Many of these activities are apparent today.

Number 4: Free trade with Communist China has already bitten us. China is stealing trade secrets and violating patents and other creative rights safeguards. This is a huge problem for our economy. The current president, Donald Trump, is trying to deal with this.

Number 6: What we are doing is a lot like aiding the enemy.

Number 7: Another case of China winning economically. President Trump is dealing with this also.

Number 11: This dream of one-world government (global government) is not going away anytime soon. This is the one where the rich gain total control, the middle class disappears, and the rest of us become "slaves" of the system. This scheme results in a dystopian world. (Dystopian is the opposite of utopian.)

Number 14: I didn't realize this was happening.

Number 15: It appears that this has already happened in the Democratic Party and is alive and well in the Republic Party to a large extent.

Number 16: This has been a huge success for the political Left. The lower courts show a blatant disregard for the Constitution.

Number 17: This is another huge success for the Left. The civics and government classes talk down the federal democracy of the United

States. The apologist administration of President Obama has made the United States the bad guy in just about every global situation.

Number 18: It appears that just about all college newspapers are way Left.

Number 19: Another win for the Left. Many universities don't allow conservative speakers. When a conservative does try to speak at a university, there are resistance groups and riots. Whatever happened to "free speech"? Can't people see what's going on? And the press presents it like the problem is the conservative speaker and his message. I fought and was willing to give my life for the rioters and the peacemakers, the Left and the Right. But the Left, like all good Marxists, doesn't allow anything but the party line. We've already lost a great deal of our right to free speech. We MUST start taking issue with this. When the press misrepresents the facts, we, the people, need to call them, write them, and hold them accountable.

Number 20: The Communists/socialists understand the importance of controlling the narrative. The best and easiest way to do that is by controlling the media. In the 1948 Soviet invasion of Czechoslovakia, one of the first buildings they seized and occupied was the national broadcasting station. From there, they gave instructions to the citizens of Czechoslovakia. In 1956, the same thing happened when they invaded Hungary. However, with America, all you need to do to control the media is buy it. The big money behind the insurgency finances demonstrations and may be responsible for the thousands of people for third-world countries massing at our borders. It was amazing to me that all the poor young people from Central American countries decided at exactly the same time to come from the country to our southern border. These masses of poor, penniless people who had brand-new clothes, luggage, tents, water bottles, and busses to transport them from one news op to another.

Number 21: This one is certainly nearing completion. Almost every radio and TV news station has an anti-democracy agenda. They, of course, cloak their agenda in high ideals and what sounds like the high moral ground, but nevertheless, the goal is to trip ordinary Americans of their right. For example, making Trump out to be a Hitler is a distraction. Generalizing the police force as "Gestapo goons" is a distortion.

Numbers 22 and 23: These two seemed to be part of the strategy during the "hippie" era. The "art" changed according to plan, but the effect was not the one the Leftists expected. The general population failed to make the association of "hippie" art with failure of our system of government. Most people who saw it felt that it was the product of marijuana. So the government embarked on the "war on drugs."

Number 24: There was definitely an effect associated with this strategy. It probably turned out better than the Leftists would have like. The Motion Picture Association rating system resulted. For the most part, the authority for enforcement was left inside the family with the parents.

Numbers 25 and 26: I think this one backfired on the Leftists. While the culture's morality level has slipped, the moral compass is still there as part of the culture, and a wave of backlash against pornography and obscenity has begun to build. Overexposure to this type of material tends to make it lose its "appeal." The fact that this material is so readily available has sadly led to some horrific crime, hence some of the backlash.

Number 27. While this objective has led to the demise of the "mainline" churches, it has led to a revitalization of service in the church. The church has a hard climb ahead of it, but it will overcome.

Number 28. This is a great example of misrepresenting intent. When we separate a few words or a phrase from its cultural and intellectual context, we also separate it from it true meaning. The Left is very skilled at changing our language as well as language of the past.

In context, "separation of church and state" is a rejection of the European model so prevalent in the 1600s and 1700s. Monarchies were empowered by the "sanction" of God. If you believed this literally, then all Monarchs had to have the approval and blessing of a high-ranking church official, like the pope or a papal representative such as a cardinal or an archbishop. It is clear from the Declaration of Independence and the Constitution that our nation was founded on the authority of a godly being. That is not a human being, be it the pope or anyone else.

Number 29. The Constitution is attacked as old-fashioned and inflexible on a daily basis. All such criticism that I have heard comes from Leftist Congress people who are attempting to pass laws that are contradictory to the Constitution. The Constitution is proven to be flexible by the very fact that there are currently twenty-seven amendments. The first ten are known as the bill of rights.

An amendment to the Constitution may be proposed by Congress or by a state. If Congress initiates the process, the amendment must first pass each house of Congress by a two-thirds majority. It then is submitted to each state where it must be ratified by the legislatures of three-quarters of the states. The alternative method is for the legislatures of three-quarters of the states to pass the amendment in ratifying conventions.[155]

Number 30. There has been a lot of this lately, but in their day, the activities were part of the culture of the day. We have disagreed with those activities, namely, slavery, and have made it illegal with the Thirteenth Amendment to the Constitution. Our culture has changed for the better. However, the failure of the previous culture does not automatically discredit every good thing accomplished during that culture. The founding fathers were schooled, intelligent men, but wealthy aristocrats is hardly a term that would fit all of them. Some of them died penniless.

Number 31. In progress at this time. Destruction of the symbols of our past is to discredit every good part of that past. Part of the problem today is that people don't understand the past because of the way it is taught—out of context. The Civil War was not fought because of slavery. It was fought over the right of a state to determine whether it would allow slavery. The war was fought over states' rights. I believe that slavery was appalling. What I am reminded of and respect when I see a statue of a Southern war hero is this. It's sad that the man believed slavery was acceptable. But I also see an American spirit of fighting and being willing to die for what you believe and for the greater good of the culture you believe in. Our way of life today is not perfect, but I have been willing to fight to the death to preserve it. So did those men in the Confederacy.

Number 34. The House Committee on Un-American Activities was dissolved in 1975. Here's what the proposed bill from the House (it failed in the senate) asserted:

Ten years of investigation by the Committee on Un-American Activities and by its predecessors have established: (1) that the Communist movement in the United States is foreign-controlled; (2) that its ultimate objective with respect to the United States is to overthrow our free American institutions in favor of a Communist totalitarian dictatorship to be controlled from abroad; (3) that its activities are carried on by secret and conspiratorial methods; and (4) that its activities, both because of the alarming march of Communist forces abroad and because of the scope and nature of Communist activities here in the United States, constitute an immediate and powerful threat to the security of the United States and to the American way of life. [156]

Number 35: The FBI leadership has discredited itself. However, the leadership was replaced, and the FBI remains one of our finest investigative organizations in our government.

Number 36: I think unions still have problems in their leadership, but I believe they are working more closely with corporate and industry leadership than ever before and in a positive manner.

Number 37. I believe that big business is looking more at global governance, which is more dystopian (socialist) than Communist.

Number 41. This one disturbs me. The pressure for both parents to work in our current culture results in the opportunity to take children from the home at a very early age and expose them to the Communist/socialist indoctrination.

Number 42. The House of Representatives is leading the way in this. Freedom of speech and freedom of thought has never justified violating those same rights of anyone who disagrees with you.

Number 43. This one sounds a lot like the "Arab Spring" movement initiated by our government under Obama and Hillary Clinton.

Number 44. The Panama Canal was not internationalized. It was given over to Panama at the end of 1999. The Panama Canal Authority remains control over it. Any country can use the canal. The three top users are the United States, China, and Japan in that order.[157]

Number 45. The global governance advocates would like to see this happen.

CLOUDS OF WAR ON THE HORIZON

Today, literally today, in the United States, we are witnessing the fruits of the labor of Leftists over the past century. Their infiltration of educational institutions, political parties, and media is evident everywhere. They have changed the meanings of words so that they are opposite what we think. For example, in American society, being a nationalist was almost synonymous with being a patriot. Now being either one is criticized as being prejudiced. If I am proud to be an American, I am considered a "nationalist" and an active opponent of all other forms of government, economy, or whatever else is different from my nation. I am called prejudiced. But by the old accepted meaning of nationalist or patriot, I was declaring a "preference," not a "prejudice." I have every right to my preferences, and so does every other person on Earth. When I begin to force my preferences on someone else, then I have a prejudice. The Leftists have replaced "preference" with "prejudice." So who is it that is trying to cram their beliefs down our throats? Is it not the Leftists?

Our Constitution is a fragile document relative to its own survival. It makes certain assumptions that are required for its existence. It requires people who love freedom in such a way that they are willing to retrain some of their own "total" freedom so that others might experience freedom. That is, people willingly limit their personal freedoms for the freedom of all. The Constitution allows us to do that by having duly elected representatives set limits that apply equally to all citizens. These limits are called laws. For the sake of the entire population, it is assumed by the Constitution that all citizens will obey the laws made by the majority of the representatives. Those who break the law have committed an offense not just against the legal system but also against the entire nation. We must always be a law-abiding nation if we are to survive as a free nation.

Our Constitution also assumes a basic education. That would be the three "Rs"—reading, "'riting," and "'rithmatics." It also assumes a fair and critical knowledge of our system of government. Public schools were, at one time, expected to require at least one American government or civics class. The word "critical" as used above meant something very different from the today's definition, or at least the practice, of "critical" by the Leftists.

The original meaning of critical in the educational process meant to examine and evaluate without prejudice. Today's meaning in the educational community seems to be an effort to discredit anything that you, the person doing the "critique," disagrees with.

The Constitution also assumes that a high percentage of the population is participating in the electoral process. As cited earlier, the average voter turnout in a presidential election is between 50 and 60 percent. Let's play a numbers game. If 60 percent of the electorate turned out to vote, then the win goes to 51 percent of the votes cast. To keep the numbers manageable, let's say the country was made up of one hundred people. Sixty of these people show up to vote. Thirty-one vote for a lower speed limit on a certain road, and twenty-nine vote against it. So the thirty-one people get their way. The other twenty-nine people have to follow the rule of the thirty-one. The other forty people who didn't vote have to follow the rule of the thirty-one as well. You can see from this that the thirty-one people have made a rule that affects the other sixty-nine people! The rule of law has been yielded to less than one-third of the people in the country! That is what happens when people who are given the right and privilege to vote don't.

If the forty people who didn't vote were unevenly divided by more than two votes, the results of the election could have been changed. True representation of the people requires all the people turning out for an election.

The born and naturalized citizens are the people who are being protected by this nation and are required to obey the laws of the nation. They, as citizens, pay taxes and receive benefits and services from those taxes. If a person is not a citizen, there are some taxes that they might pay because there are many government services that apply to all indiscriminately. National parks, highways, buildings, police protection, etc., are just a few. Because elections directly affect our lives as citizens, only citizens should vote and only vote once, and photo ID should be required.

Citizens should participate in political parties, at least to some degree. Citizens should visit the local office of their congressional representative at least once a year and the local office of their two senators at least once a year. Anytime a citizen is particularly pleased or displeased with the way one of them voted, their office should be visited by the citizen.

Under the Constitution as we know it, citizens are expected to obey the laws that are duly made. If a citizen disagrees with a law, the amendments of the Constitution allow that person or persons to gather in public and express, in a civil manner and without breaking any laws, their opposition to a law or a proposed law. So they are allowed to gather; to speak their minds, hopefully in an intelligent and decent manner; and even to bear arms within the constraints of the local laws.

So today in Seattle, a group of Leftists, anarchists, and others are claiming property that legally belongs to other people not interested in their movement. They claim to be protesting against a brutal murder committed by a white policeman on a black man. To be upset and demand justice for the black man and punishment for the policeman is justified simply because it is a murder. The policeman demonstrated his bad nature and poor character by committing the act. There's a law against it, he has been arrested under the law, and I trust that he will be punished by way of due process under the law.

The reaction of the Left who would undermine our Constitution was to break the very laws they would like to see enforced and to claim exemption from the law themselves, even as they infringe on the rights of the good people who live in the area that they seized. When they get mad, they think they are above the law. But when laws are broken, regardless of who broke them, due process, including "innocent until proven guilty," should be applied. We as citizens must demand this. We must be a nation of laws and a nation of law-abiding citizens. Changing the laws is a constitutional option. Ignoring them is not.

It is not the role of citizens to punish the lawbreakers. We have law enforcement people whose job it is to catch lawbreakers and judges and courts to determine their guilt or innocence based on the evidence presented and the appropriate level of punishment, if the accused is determined to be guilty of the charges. Anything less than this due process is vigilante activity—taking the law into your own hands—and is illegal and can be prosecuted under the law. Does this system work all the time? No! But it is better than any other country has.

One of the things I've observed in this encounter is how quickly the Leftists "profile." I thought they were against that. But apparently, if you wear a police uniform, you are profiled as "bad" automatically and racist. Isn't that a clear case of hypocrisy?

Another thing that bothers me is the crime and vandalism that occurs in these "protests." My question is, if a person who is protesting against lawbreakers or someone that they perceive to be a lawbreaker, don't they see that when they break the law in their protest, they, too, have become a lawbreaker? There is no difference between them and the person they are protesting against. They're both breaking the law in total disregard for the law and the good citizens of the nation. They are both lawbreakers. This leads me to conclude that their protests are not even about the law! It's about overthrow of the law and, in some cases, the whole principle of law. Or they are people with a bigger agenda and simply creating chaos!

It is time for the justice system to start exercising its legal authority to fulfill their obligations where laws are broken while at the same time not abusing their legal power. The rule concerning use of force or power has always been, and should remain, to restrain from using any force beyond the minimum needed to address the threat. If that minimum is exceeded, the person or persons involved should be punished and retrained, if not fired. A law enforcement officer is absolutely not THE law. They all need to be reminded of this periodically.

What changes are needed? I've already mentioned the recognition of the real threat we are dealing with in this country. It's not every person who breaks the law. It's the people who want to destroy the law and the order in this country. It's about revolution, and they even have started using that word.

So the first thing we need to do is help people recognize the intent of these protesters. This movement to overthrow our government began as outside influences attempting to create a revolt—textbook Marxism. We need to, at some point, stand up to these protesters with demonstrations of our own but execute these demonstrations in an orderly, legal manner. The abusive protesters don't care if we

JERRY L. BURTON

lose this right because they don't care about rights. They will always do what they want and try to justify themselves by blaming some segment of society they don't like.

The next thing we need to do is start showing our presence in the school system. We need to get the propaganda out of the classroom. Parents need to look at every textbook their child is using. And parents need to be very vocal about objectionable content. If necessary, form your own parent advisory council and go to the school board meetings and respectfully ask questions and, if necessary, make demands. Don't be afraid to "take names and threaten to kick," you know what, at the net election. Take good notes or record on tape or video what you say and how you say it so you can fairly your discussion to whoever might be interested. If the school begins to take your behavior and complaints out on your child, find a sympathetic lawyer who will write a threatening letter for you. It would be best if you can find a parent who is a lawyer and willing to be a part of you parent advisory council.

We need to recognize that our voice is not being recognized by the media or Congress. I've already talked about the need for our presence in the halls of our government. But the media has sold us out. When Nixon was forced out of the Oval Office for lying and covering up the Watergate break-in, he lost the confidence of the people who had put him into office. The fact that two reporters could bring down a sitting president went to the heads of the media. Their interpretation of Watergate was that they had achieved the power to determine who held office and who stayed in office. The media has been misleading and bypassing the people of the United States ever since. The media has become obsessed with itself, betrayed the public, and become worse than Richard Nixon ever was. We need to fill the "Letters to the Editor" inbox!

We need to provide less money to the government and more money to charitable institutions and churches so that people who can't help themselves have a place to go to get help. And we need to create a way to make all these institutions, including our government, accountable for every penny we give them. Maybe a "private citizen" version of the IRS! Part of the monitoring of the elected members of our government should be a mandatory audit of each person before they enter their office. The audit should be done by a nongovernment audit firm. From the audit, their net worth should be determined, and that number should be made public the day they enter office. Another audit should be done each year, not by the same audit firm who did the entry audit. This number should also be made public. The net gain or loss should be published along with the amount of government pay and benefits they received each year they were in office. Corruption within Congress and the other branches of our government must be challenged, tried, and punished heavily! Every elected official should fear violating the confidence of the people who elected them.

Also, term limits need to be put in place. I don't believe our founding fathers ever intended an elected office become a "career" position.

These things I've just discussed are all war clouds on the horizon. We can act now to change things, or we will pay the price in defeat later.

We are under attack from within. There is no other country on Earth like ours. There is no other country on Earth that is not envious of us. We are the beacon of light on the hill. Take us out and the whole world will suffer. They think that they can replace us and have what we have. The honor and integrity of their leaders is worse than the "capitalists" they call evil. Even China has become capitalistic, but it still enslaves its people in the process. Have you seen any demonstrations demanding a higher minimum wage in China? Have you seen any demonstrations in any communist country at all? Not many, I'd bet. And if you do see more than one demonstration in those countries, you won't see the same people; they will have all disappeared.

Communism is just a term. Its meaning changes as often as our enemies need to change it. Communism, socialism, democratic socialism, progressivism, it doesn't matter. It all means the same thing: getting rid of our "Government of the People, by the People, and for the People." And by the way, that phrase did not originate with Abraham Lincoln, nor with the founding fathers, nor with Daniel Webster. It is thought that the first use of this phrase may have appeared in 1384 in the prologue of John Wycliffe's first printing of the complete Bible in English—"This Bible is for the Government of the People, by the People, and for the People."[158]

This discussion would not be complete without taking a look at the personal life and perhaps the motives of Karl Marx.

KARL MARX – THE MAN[159]

Karl Marx was one of nine children. His father was a successful lawyer, so they had money and influence. Europe was infatuated with social theory at the time. The academic world referred to it as the "Age of Enlightenment."

Marx was an average student. His first year in college, at the University of Bonn, was disastrous. He was there for only two semesters. During that time, he was thrown in prison for drunkenness and disturbing the peace. He incurred substantial debts and participated in a duel. His father made him enroll in the University of Berlin. Marx eventually received a doctorate from the University of Jena.

Marx married a high-society woman from a very wealthy family, Jenny von Westphalen. She was four years older than he was, and neither set of parents approved of the union. He and Jenny had seven children. He and the "nanny" had one. Of Jenny's seven children, only three survived. Two of the surviving girls later committed suicide.[160]

Marx was too radical even for the universities. None would hire him. So he worked as a journalist and author. There were radicals who liked his writing, but they didn't pay him. Governments didn't like him or his writings, so he got to see France, Belgium, and England.

In France, Marx was introduced to Communism. Note that Marx did not "father" Communism. He met Friedrich Engels. Engels was actually from England, but the two decided to collaborate. Marx didn't have any money, so Engels began funding him. This makes it sound like Engels had money, but nothing he did made money either. He actually survived by working in a factory owned by his father.

Because of Marx's radical Communist writing, France threw him out. From France, Marx and Jenny went to Belgium.

In Brussels, he met Moses Hess, who introduced him to Socialism. Marx then left the Communist League. Marx wrote several works in Brussels, but they were so radical that no one wanted to publish them.

Marx did, however, form a Communist Correspondence Committee to coordinate the writings of socialists around Europe. The socialists in England formed a Communist League and asked Marx and Engels to write what came to be known as *The Communist Manifesto*. Marx and Engels collaborated and wrote the *Manifesto*, not Marx by himself. Shortly thereafter, Marx was expelled from Belgium.

Marx went to London, formed the headquarters for the Communist League, and worked as a journalist. In 1867, Marx published the first volume of *Das Kapital*. Engels completed the last two volumes after Marx died using Marx's notes to a large extent.

Karl Marx never earned a living wage and was supported almost entirely by Engels.

My Thoughts on "Marxism"

Das Kapital, as I recall, was largely a critique of capitalism and the associated exploitation. I have to remind myself that this writing was framed by the initial stages of the Industrial Revolution. Marx took the position that capitalism was immoral and that profits were unsustainable. His major criticism was the management of commodities. In my opinion, Marx was largely correct in a restricted environment. However, in an expanding world economy, which we had by the end of World War I, he was wrong. Not only did the profitability increase, but capitalism also gave birth to a new middle class.

JERRY L. BURTON

Every place the socialists, Communists, anti-capitalists, whatever you want to call them took over, the government officials took the place of the "rotten capitalists," and the poor worker got poorer and had even less access to the bare necessities than previously. That can be seen in the real practice, not just theory. China is a great example of a "Communist" dictatorship that could not advance until it shifted over to capitalism. The difference between China and the United States economically is that as the economy in the United States improves; every class—upper, middle, and lower—also improves. In China, the upper, dictatorial rulers get richer, a wealthy middle class has emerged, but the lower class is still receiving "Communist" wages. There are, just my guess, probably more people in China being exploited than any other country on Earth today. Communist and socialist dictatorships today exploit exponentially more people than capitalistic democracies.

We MUST stand up to those powers who want to destroy our way of life. And we need to stand up and change those things that beg to be changed. There is not now, nor will there ever be, a better form of government than we have under our Constitution. We need to protect it and change it only by the people and for the people. We, non-Communists and nonsocialists, are the people, and we are the majority. When we vote, we save our country. Complacency will lose our country!

TURNING FINAL

As a B-24 pilot, I had one airplane and one mission. What difference could I make?

I knew that I could not win the war by myself. But I also had confidence in the other pilots and crews. I knew they would do their part, even if it killed them. And it did kill quite a few of them.

My job was to do the job assigned to me to best of my ability. And I did. Every flight made was another pilot and crew just doing their job to preserve the freedoms we enjoy as a nation.

If we are to continue as a one nation, under God, then every true American needs to step up—now. Like me, you will just be one person. But if you work, others will work, and together, we can save our way of life for generations to come.

As for me,

> *I will never forget that I am an American fighting for freedom, responsible for my actions, and dedicated to the principles that made my country free. I will trust in my God and in the United States of America.*

This is Bill Drumm, turning final and passing the torch to you. God's speed!

JERRY L. BURTON

NOTES

1   "The Charge of the Light Brigade," Alfred Lord Tennyson, 1854.

2   https://www.britannica.com/place/Ottoman-Empire

3   https://www.historic-uk.com/HistoryUK/HistoryofBritain/Timeline-Of-The-British-Empire/

4   https://about-history.com/history-of-the-german-empire-1871-1918/

5   http://socialstudiesforkids.com/articles/worldhistory/austro-hungarianempire.htm

6   https://thesoundingline.com/map-of-the-day-the-rise-and-fall-of-the-french-empire/

7   https://www.worldatlas.com/articles/what-was-the-russian-empire.html

8   ibid.

9   https://worldhistory.us/chinese-history/the-opium-war-and-the-opening-of-china.php

10 Gill, N.S. "The Fall of Rome: How, When, and Why Did It Happen?" ThoughtCo.   https://www.thoughtco.com/what-was-the-fall-of-rome-112688 (accessed May 11, 2020).

11 https://www.history.com/this-day-in-history/austria-hungary-annexes-bosnia-herzegovina

12 https://ian.macky.net/pat/map/seur/seurblk2.gif

13 Citation: C N Trueman "Italy and World War One" historylearningsite.co.uk. The History Learning Site, 25 May 2015. 18 Dec 2019.

14 The Editors of Encyclopaedia Britannica; Zimmermann Telegram; Encyclopædia Britannica; Encyclopædia Britannica, inc.; Published: December 18, 2019; https://www.britannica.com/event/Zimmermann-Telegram; Accessed: March 30, 2020

15 https://www.timetoast.com/timelines/117937

16 https://www.history.com/this-day-in-history/america-enters-world-war-i

17 https://www.timetoast.com/timelines/117937

18 https://www.dummies.com/education/history/american-history/
   u-s-economy-and-industry-during-world-war-ii/
19 https://blog.timesunion.com/history/rainbow-division-got-its-
   start-100-years-ago/2276/
20 https://firstworldwar.com/atoz/rainbowdivision.htm
21 U.S., Army Transport Service, Passenger Lists, 1910-1939
22 https://www.historycentral.com/ww1/Stmichiel.html
23 U.S., Army Transport Service, Passenger Lists, 1910-1939
24 U.S., Army Transport Service, Passenger Lists, 1910-1939
25 https://history.army.mil/html/forcestruc/lineages/branches/fa/0151fa.htm
26 U.S., Army Transport Service, Passenger Lists, 1910-1939
27 https://e-anca.org/History/Topics-in-ANC-History/
   Contributions-of-the-US-Army-Nurse-Corps-in-WWI
28 https://history.amedd.army.mil/booksdocs/wwi/adminamerexp/chapter23.
   html; Information presented on this service not identified as protected by
   copyright is considered public information and may be distributed or copied.
   Use of appropriate byline, photo, and image credits is requested.
29 ibid.
30 ibid.
31 http://www.worldwar1.com/dbc/basehosp.htm
32 U.S., Army Transport Service, Passenger Lists, 1910-1939
33 https://history.amedd.army.mil/booksdocs/wwi/adminamerexp/chapter24.
   html; Information presented on this service not identified as protected by
   copyright is considered public information and may be distributed or copied.
   Use of appropriate byline, photo, and image credits is requested.
34 "Japan gives ultimatum to Germany"; History.com Editors; HISTORY;
   https://www.history.com/this-day-in-history/japan-gives-ultimatum-to-
   germany; Access Date: March 21, 2020; A&E Television Networks; Last
   Updated: August 14, 2019; Original Published Date: November 16, 2009
35 https://www.history.com/this-day-in-history/japan-gives-ultimatum-
   to-germany
36 http://countrystudies.us/japan/29.htm; Source: *U.S. Library of Congress*
37 "China declares war on Germany "; History.com Editors; HISTORY;
   https://www.history.com/this-day-in-history/china-declares-war-on-
   germany; Access Date: March 21, 2020; A&E Television Networks; Last
   Updated: August 13, 2019; Original Published Date: November 5, 2009
38 https://encyclopedia.ushmm.org/content/en/map/german-territorial-
   losses-treaty-of-versailles-1919
39 "Treaty of Versailles"; History.com Editors; HISTORY; https://www.
   history.com/topics/world-war-i/treaty-of-versailles-1; Access Date: March
   21, 2020; A&E Television Networks; Last Updated: March 3, 2020; Original

Published Date: October 29, 2009

40 https://genius.com/Irving-berlin-blue-skies-lyrics

41 https://www.thebalance.com/roaring-twenties-4060511

42 https:// allthatsinteresting.com/famous-gangsters-1920s#9

43 http://www.fsmitha.com/time/1928.htm

44 https://www.politico.com/story/2013/05/this-day-in-politics-091600

45 https://www.history.com/this-day-in-history/the-grand-ole-opry-begins-broadcasting, accessed 2/10/2020

46 https://historynewsnetwork.org/blog/14513

47 https://reelrundown.com/film-industry/Hollywood_-_The_History_of_a_Movie_Capital

48 https://cleancomedians.com/the-history-of-comedy-1920-to-2020/

49 https://video.search.yahoo.com/search/video?p=Will+Rogers#id=3&vid=591dfe8e36e0576e5d5007e416eebf89&action=view

50 https://www.legendsofamerica.com/66-timeline/

51 http://www.fsmitha.com/time/1927.htm

52 http://www.fsmitha.com/time/1928.htm

53 ibid.

54 https://www.census.gov/history/www/through_the_decades/fast_facts/1920_fast_facts.html

55 Article Title: Walt Disney Biography; Author: Biography.com Editors; Website Name: The Biography.com website; URL: https://www.biography.com/business-figure/walt-disney; Access Date: April 27, 2020; Publisher: A&E Television Networks; Last Updated: August 21, 2019; Original Published Date: April 2, 2014

56 https://www.history.com/topics/great-depression/dust-bowl

57 "Weimar Republic timeline: 1921-23"; Jennifer Llewellyn, Brian Doone, Jim Southey, Steve Thompson; Alpha History; https://alphahistory.com/weimarrepublic/weimar-republic-timeline-1921-23/; Date published: February 10, 2018; Date accessed: April 04, 2020

58 https://worldhistoryproject.org/1921

59 The Editors of Encyclopaedia Britannica; "Traudl Junge"; Encyclopædia Britannica; Encyclopædia Britannica, inc.; Date Published: March 12, 2020; https://www.britannica.com/biography/Traudl-Junge; Access Date: April 05, 2020

60 "American assistance to Weimar Germany"; Jennifer Llewellyn, Steve Thompson; Alpha History; https://alphahistory.com/weimarrepublic/american-assistance/; Date published: September 30, 2019; Date accessed: April 05, 2020

61 "The Spanish Civil War"; Jennifer Llewellyn, Jim Southey, Steve Thompson; Alpha History; https://alphahistory.com/nazigermany/spanish-civil-war/;

Date published: September 1, 2015; Date accessed: April 02, 2020

62 https://www.history.com/topics/world-war-ii/benito-mussolini

63 "Vladimir Lenin"; History.com Editors; HISTORY; https://www.history.com/topics/russia/vladimir-lenin; Access Date: April 7, 2020; Publisher: A&E Television Networks; Last Updated: March 5, 2020; Original Published Date: November 9, 2009

64 "9 Things You May Not Know About Vladimir Lenin"; Jesse Greenspan; HISTORY; https://www.history.com/news/9-things-you-may-not-know-about-vladimir-lenin; Access Date: May 13, 2020; Publisher: A&E Television Networks; Last Updated: September 4, 2018; Original Published Date: January 21, 2014

65 "Vladimir Lenin"; History.com Editors; HISTORY; https://www.history.com/topics/russia/vladimir-lenin; Access Date: April 7, 2020; Publisher: A&E Television Networks; Last Updated: March 5, 2020; Original Published Date: November 9, 2009

66 The Editors of Encyclopaedia Britannica; "Communist Party of the Soviet Union"; Encyclopædia Britannica; Publisher: Encyclopædia; Britannica, inc.; Date Published: April 26, 2018; URL: https://www.britannica.com/topic/Communist-Party-of-the-Soviet-Union; Access Date: April 07, 2020

67 "Vladimir Lenin"; History.com Editors; HISTORY; https://www.history.com/topics/russia/vladimir-lenin; Access Date: April 7, 2020; Publisher: A&E Television Networks; Last Updated: March 5, 2020; Original Published Date: November 9, 2009

68 ibid.

69 ibid.

70 ibid.

71 ibid.

72 http://motherearthtravel.com/history/japan/history-9.htm

73 ibid.

74 McElroy, Joe. Relations Between Japan & the USA in the 1930s & 1940s last modified May 9, 2020. https://classroom.synonym.com/relations-between-japan-usa-1930s-1940s-20938.html

75 The Editors of Encyclopaedia Britannica; Second Sino-Japanese War; Encyclopædia Britannica; Publisher: Encyclopædia Britannica, inc.; Date Published: March 14, 2019; URL: https://www.britannica.com/event/Second-Sino-Japanese-War; Access Date: May 09, 2020

76 "Germany annexes Austria"; History.com Editors; HISTORY; https://www.history.com/this-day-in-history/germany-annexes-austria; Access Date: April 5, 2020; Publisher: A&E Television Networks; Last Updated: March 10, 2020; Original Published Date: February 9, 2010

77 https://www.timetoast.com/timelines/events-between-ww1-and-ww2

78 Rosenberg, Jennifer. "The Nazi-Soviet Non-Aggression Pact." ThoughtCo, Mar. 30, 2020, thoughtco.com/nazi-soviet-non-aggression-pact-1779994.

79 "Germans invade Poland"; History.com Editors; HISTORY; https://www.history.com/this-day-in-history/germans-invade-poland; Access Date: April 5, 2020; Publisher: A&E Television Networks; Last Updated: July 28, 2019; Original Published Date: March 4, 2010

80 Rosenberg, Jennifer. "Timeline of World War II From 1939 to 1945." ThoughtCo, Feb. 18, 2020, thoughtco.com/world-war-ii-timeline-1779991

81 http://www.worldwar2facts.org/axis-powers.html

82 https://www.history.com/topics/world-war-ii/dunkirk

83 https://www.warhistoryonline.com/world-war-ii/10-countries-invaded-fascist-italy-invaded-one.html

84 History.com Editors; HISTORY; https://www.history.com/this-day-in-history/tide-turns-in-the-battle-of-britain; Access Date: May 4, 2020; Publisher: A&E Television Networks; Last Updated: July 28, 2019; Original Published Date: March 4, 2010

85 https://www.warhistoryonline.com/world-war-ii/10-countries-invaded-fascist-italy-invaded-one.html

86 Rosenberg, Jennifer. "Timeline of World War II From 1939 to 1945." ThoughtCo, Feb. 18, 2020, thoughtco.com/world-war-ii-timeline-1779991

87 https://www.warhistoryonline.com/world-war-ii/10-countries-invaded-fascist-italy-invaded-one.html

88 89 Lend-Lease Act; History.com Editors; HISTORY; https://www.history.com/topics/world-war-ii/lend-lease-act-1; Access Date: June 3, 2020; A&E Television Networks; Last Updated: November 4, 2019; Original Published Date: October 29, 2009

89 https://www.warhistoryonline.com/world-war-ii/10-countries-invaded-fascist-italy-invaded-one.html

90 http://www.historyplace.com/unitedstates/pacificwar/timeline.htm

91 Rickard, J (2 September 2009), *Japanese conquest of Burma, December 1941-May 1942,* http://www.historyofwar.org/articles/campaign_burma_japanese.html

92 Hickman, Kennedy. "World War II: Battle of Hong Kong." ThoughtCo, Feb. 11, 2020, thoughtco.com/battle-of-hong-kong-2361469.

93 https://www.businessinsider.com/battle-of-attu-and-kiska-in-alaska-us-japanese-troops-in-north-america-2018-5

94 Michael Ray; Battle of Midway; Encyclopædia Britannica; Encyclopædia Britannica, inc.; Date Published: May 27, 2020; https://www.britannica.com/event/Battle-of-Midway; Access Date: June 20, 2020

95 The Editors of Encyclopaedia Britannica; Battle of Guadalcanal; Encyclopædia Britannica; Encyclopædia Britannica, inc.; Date Published: December 15,

2016; https://www.britannica.com/event/Battle-of-Guadalcanal; Access Date: June 20, 2020

96 http://ww2today.com/24th-january-1943-roosevelt-calls-for-unconditional-surrender

97 Battle of Stalingrad; History.com Editors; HISTORY; https://www.history.com/topics/world-war-ii/battle-of-stalingrad; Access Date: May 13, 2020; A&E Television Networks; Last Updated: August 28, 2019; Original Published Date: November 9, 2009

98 The Battle of the Bismarck Sea; History.com Editors; HISTORY; https://www.history.com/this-day-in-history/the-battle-of-the-bismarck-sea; Access Date: June 20, 2020; Publisher: A&E Television Networks; Last Updated: February 28, 2020; Original Published Date: November 16, 2009

99 Rickard, J (19 November 2014), *Battle of the Philippine Sea, 19-20 June 1944,* http://www.historyofwar.org/articles/battles_philippine_sea.html

100 https://www.atomicheritage.org/location/oak-ridge-tn

101 Contributor: The Editors of Encyclopaedia Britannica; Article Title: Battle of Leyte Gulf; Website Name: Encyclopædia Britannica; Publisher: Encyclopædia Britannica, inc.; Date Published: October 16, 2019; URL: https://www.britannica.com/event/Battle-of-Leyte-Gulf; Access Date: May 14, 2020

102 https://onlineutah.us/wendoverairfieldhistory_06.shtml

103 https://www.historynet.com/battle-of-the-bulge

104 https://www.militaryfactory.com/aircraft/ww2-japanese-kamikaze-aircraft.asp

105 https://warfarehistorynetwork.com/2016/09/07/operation-matterhorn/

106 http://www.cbi-history.com/part_vi_20th_af-1.html

107 http://www.cbi-theater.com/matterhorn/matterhorn.html

108 https://warfarehistorynetwork.com/2016/09/07/operation-matterhorn/

109 https://www.armyaircorpsmuseum.org/308th_Bombardment_Group.cfm

110 Crash sites are still being found, seventy-even years after they aircraft disappeared. MIA Recoveries, Inc.; https://www.miarecoveries.org/reports/

111 https://www.pbs.org/wgbh/americanexperience/features/truman-leaflets/

112 https://www.cia.gov/library/center-for-the-study-of-intelligence/csi-publications/csi-studies/studies/vol46no3/article07.html

113 Japan accepts Potsdam terms, agrees to unconditional surrender; History.com Editors; HISTORY; https://www.history.com/this-day-in-history/japan-accepts-potsdam-terms-agrees-to-unconditional-surrender; Access Date: July 21, 2020; A&E Television Networks; Last Updated: August 7, 2019; Original Published Date: November 5, 2009

114 https://www.npr.org/templates/story/story.php?storyId=4785786

115 http://www.american-historama.org/1945-1989-cold-war-era/

potsdam-conference.htm

116 Flight of the Enola Gay, Paul W. Tibbets, Copyright @ Paul W. Tibbets

117 https://www.britannica.com/place/Germany/The-era-of-partition

118 https://www.history.com/this-day-in-history/soviets-blockade-west-berlin

119 https://medium.com/war-is-boring/the-hump-was-the-deadliest-cargo-flight-in-history-13fe4ff5a09

120 https://www.nationalcoldwarexhibition.org/schools-colleges/national-curriculum/berlin-airlift/facts-figures.aspx

121 https://www.britannica.com/event/Berlin-blockade

122 https://www.britannica.com/list/korean-war-timeline

123 https://www.cafsocal.com/our-aircrafts/our-aircraft-and-history/north-american-snj-5-texan/

124 https://www.afhra.af.mil/Portals/16/documents/Timelines/Korea/KoreanWarChronology.pdf?ver=2016-08-30-151058-710

125 https://video.search.yahoo.com/search/video?p=nuclear+tests+men+in+trenches#id=2&vid=b60d945ce214848c83dffd4d89c70b9a&action=click

126 https://www.dtra.mil/Portals/61/Documents/NTPR/1-Fact_Sheets/16_TEAPOT.pdf; Page 4

127 http://www.radiochemistry.org/history/nuke_tests/teapot/index.html

128 https://history.state.gov/milestones/1945-1952/national-security-act

129 https://www.heritage.org/defense/report/us-nuclear-weapons-europe-critical-transatlantic-security

130 http://www.designation-systems.net/dusrm/m-19.html

131 https://www.history.com/news/kennedy-krushchev-vienna-summit-meeting-1961

132 https://alphahistory.com/coldwar/khrushchevs-letter-to-kennedy-on-cuba-1962/

133 https://nsarchive2.gwu.edu/nsa/cuba_mis_cri/moment.htm

134 ibid.

135 Nikita Khrushchev; History.com Editors; HISTORY; https://www.history.com/topics/cold-war/nikita-sergeyevich-khrushchev; Access Date: June 8, 2020; Publisher: A&E Television Networks; Last Updated: March 29, 2019; Original Published Date: November 9, 2009

136 https://www.thoughtco.com/what-was-french-indochina-195328

137 https://www.thoughtco.com/ho-chi-minh-195778

138 https://www.warhistoryonline.com/vietnam-war/cu-chi-tunnels-dangerous-underground-warzone.html

139 https://www.goodfreephotos.com/albums/united-states/louisiana/new-orleans/new-orleans-louisiana-after-the-flooding-of-hurricane-katrina.jpg

140 https://www.goodfreephotos.com/albums/united-states/mississippi/other-mississippi/hurricane-katrina-in-bay-st-louis-mississippi.jpg

141 https://www.army.mil/values/oath.html

142 https://liberalsarenuts.com/2017/12/24/the-naked-communist-45-goals-to-destroy-the-united-states-of-america/

143 https://www.worldometers.info/world-population/us-population/

144 https://www.federalregister.gov/documents/2019/10/04/2019-21663/estimates-of-the-voting-age-population-for-2018

145 https://ballotpedia.org/Voter_turnout_in_United_States_elections

146 ibid.

147 ibid.

148 https://www.statista.com/statistics/262915/voter-turnout-in-the-us-presidential-elections/

149 https://worldpopulationreview.com/states/voter-turnout-by-state/

150 https://ballotpedia.org/Voter_turnout_in_United_States_elections

151 ibid.

152 https://www.sos.state.nm.us/voting-and-elections/data-and-maps/voter-registration-statistics/2019-voter-registration-statistics/

153 https://nmpolitics.net/index/2017/02/voter-turnout-was-up-in-first-nm-elections-since-trumps-win/

154 https://worldpopulationreview.com/states/voter-turnout-by-state/

155 The Editors of Encyclopaedia_Britannica; List of amendments to the U.S. Constitution; Encyclopædia Britannica; Encyclopædia Britannica, inc.; Date Published: August 27, 2014; URL: https://www.britannica.com/topic/list-of-amendments-to-the-U-S-Constitution-1787122; Access Date: June 15, 2020

156 The Editors of Encyclopaedia Britannica; House Un-American Activities Committee; Encyclopædia Britannica; Encyclopædia Britannica, inc.; Date Published: January 28, 2020; https://www.britannica.com/topic/House-Un-American-Activities-Committee; Access Date: June 15, 2020

157 http://www.pancanal.com/eng/

158 https://www.bookbrowse.com/expressions/detail/index.cfm/expression_number/600/government-of-the-people-by-the-people-for-the-people

159 https://www.biography.com/scholar/karl-marx; Access Date: June 21, 2020; Publisher: A&E Television Networks; Last Updated: April 17, 2020; Original Published Date: April 2, 2014

160 https://www.psychologytoday.com/us/blog/creating-in-flow/201203/5-fascinating-facts-about-karl-marxs-wife

William H. Drumm, Sr.

WWI, France
Rainbow Division

Pvt, Company C, 106th Field Signal Battalion

PFC, Hdqtrs, 151st Field Artillery

Luther G. Maloney
Rainbow Division, France

Pvt, CO A, 140th Regiment of Infantry
Raids against Germans in the Vosges Mountains; St. Mihiel largest battle involving AEFs.

Purple Heart.

Cpl, Hdqtrs, 151st Field Artillery

Aunt Sadie

US Army Nurse Corps

France

Sadie A. Krause
US Army Nurse Corps

LTC William E. Drumm, Jr.
MBA

USAAF, USAF

WWII, Pilot B-24, CBI
Berlin Blockade, Stateside
AIRE,
Korea (Japan, ACRW)

German, Comptroller

LT. COL. BILL DRUMM U.S.A.
U.S. AIRFORCE

Brother, Bob

LTC Robert Drumm

USAAF, USAF

Cousin Bernice "Doll"

US Navy WAVE

Served in DC

David Drumm

US Army

Medical Administration

Col. Robert H. Drumm, Jr.

West Point Grad.

Black Hawk Pilot

South Korea DMZ

We pledged allegiance to our flag.
We took the oath to protect our Constitution against all enemies, foreign and domestic.
For over 100 years we have been Americans fighting for our country and our way of life.
We have been, and are, willing to give our lives in their defense!

Michael J. Drumm

U.S. Air Force

Honorable AIRTEC

LTC Michael W. Drumm, Sr.

Son of Robert Drumm

US Army Pilot: O-1 Mohawk

Bosnia, Kosovo
CO of Intel Sqden in Iraq

Father of US Marine, US Navy SEAL, Michael (Mikie) W. Drumm, Jr.

Michael (Mikie) W. Drumm, Jr.

U.S. Marines

U.S. Navy - SEAL

Capt Dan of Chapman and wife Martha, Bill Drumm's daughter.

David was a graduate of the US Air Force Academy.

After the Air Force, he became a pilot with Delta Airlines.

Capt Sean Chapman, son of David Chapman and Bill's daughter, Martha.

US Army, Air Medivac

Afghanistan

Inscription reads:
Hi Grandpa
I'm staying true to the family business!

Sherrie Drumm, wife of "Mikie" Drumm, Jr.

U.S. Coast Guard

Lightning Source UK Ltd.
Milton Keynes UK
UKHW011039200820
368549UK00002B/234/J

9 781664 121737